When in Doubt . . .

When in Doubt . . .

The Faith Journeys of Young Adults

Richard H. Hill

Bridge Resources
Louisville, Kentucky

Edited by David M. Dobson

Book and cover design by Claire Calhoun

First edition

Published by Bridge Resources
Louisville, Kentucky

Web site address: http://www.bridgeresources.org

PRINTED IN THE UNITED STATES OF AMERICA

99 00 01 02 03 04 05 06 07 08 — 10 9 8 7 6 5 4 3 2 1

Library of Congress Cataloging-in-Publication Data

Hill, Richard H., date.
When in doubt— : the faith journeys of young adults / Richard H. Hill — 1st ed.
p. cm.
Includes bibliographical references.
ISBN 1-57895-072-4
1. College students—Religious life—United States. 2. Christian college students—Religious life—United States. I. Title.
BL625.9.C64H55 1999
200'. 84'2—dc21 98-43700

Contents

Introduction 1

1. An End to Childish Ways 5

2. Trouble in the Church 21

3. Where Is the Flock? 35

4. The Cry for Insight 51

5. What Is "Success"? 67

6. Wrestling with God 81

7. "*I AM* Has Sent Me to You" 95

8. Equipped for Every Good Work 111

9. Resources 127

About the Author 137

Introduction

I knew a man, he used to sit in the corner.
He hid every time someone shook a finger.
Then one day he got tired of watchin'
Life goin' by like a big screen drive-in.
He said to himself, "I gotta quit this cryin',
I'll be what I wanna be—I'll be on a roll!"
—Rick Hill, "See What You Wanna See"

I have been a campus minister for seven years. In that time I have come to the conclusion that most people have no idea of where college students are in their faith journeys. Ministers, campus ministers, even parents really had no idea of what was going on with the college students. I didn't really know either, which made my job very frustrating. Being at a state school, I found the university wasn't terribly interested in anything having to do with faith, and so had very few resources. This only added to my frustration, because I have felt for a long time that faith serves as the basis for everything we do.

Several of my colleagues have taken sabbaticals in their seventh year and I decided to do the same. The subject for my sabbatical was "The Faith Journeys of College Students." I just really had to find out what was going on. I spent three months talking with students in seven states on thirteen different campuses, both private and public. I was mainly interested in talking with Christian students, because I wanted to find out why they weren't participating in campus ministries and attending church. But I decided to check out what was happening in other religions as well to see if this was just a "Christian thing" or if this was a general condition of this age group. So I interviewed Christians, Jews, Muslims, Hindus, Wiccans, pagans, several agnostics, and one or two atheists. I interviewed about seventy-five students, both males and females, from a variety of cultures and races.

The interviews lasted anywhere from forty-five minutes to two hours. The students would first tell me about their faith journeys from as far back as they could remember, and then they would answer a set of questions that I developed partially from James Fowler's Faith Development questions and mostly from my own curiosity. Some of their faith stories are in chapter 3, some of their answers to the questions are in chapter 4. Other bits and pieces of those interviews are scattered throughout the book. (These stories are identified by three small squares that appear above and below each excerpt.) I would have loved to include every word they said, but that would take up volumes. Some of their stories are heart-wrenching, some are maddening, some are just plain disturbing. But they are real stories of real people trying to make sense out of their life experiences.

The individual beliefs presented in the quotes may or may not be the actual doctrine of any given religion. These are the ways the students have experienced the congregation or the religion they have been involved with and the meaning they have drawn from that experience. This is not a study in world religions. These are words that come from the heart.

I have a special leaning toward those who have become disenchanted with the church because I have struggled for years with a love/hate relationship with the institution. Though I felt the church in which I grew up was often warm and caring, I have also felt betrayed as I've watched churches turn their backs on people who were suffering or in need, sometimes even their own members! I have been involved with churches who have split over leadership disputes, churches who have struggled to do the work of Christ but have grown weary, churches whose only desire is to die a peaceful death. And I try to make some sense of it all.

Several years ago I went through a serious crisis of faith. I had felt it growing for years, and it finally came to a head when my beliefs were questioned, my faith was doubted by a colleague. I was filled with doubts and questions, but everywhere I turned I got the feeling that I was not supposed to be having doubts and questions. This, of course, only made matters worse. For six months I went through sleepless nights and fearful days, asking God over and over for some insight, some answer that would reassure me.

As I searched, I went to conferences, read books, and talked with ministers and others. And in each place, in each conversation, I began to get some of the answers I was looking for and some that were totally unexpected. God answered my pleas and put me in contact with people who helped me gain some clarity again.

I continue to have questions and doubts. But I have a better sense of how to handle them, and I always keep my eyes and ears open to the wisdom that God sends through others.

This book is for those who are doubting, for those who struggle with the faith that has been handed to them. Doubting is one of the best things you can do, even though it can be absolute hell. And one of the worst things the church can do is to turn away the doubters. We do not lose our faith because of our doubts, we grow in our faith because of them.

This book moves in four steps. First, I will discuss my research, focusing primarily on the developmental theories of James Fowler and Sharon Parks. Then I will share portions of the interviews and show where the students are currently in their faith journeys. Third, I will discuss the implications of this research for both campus ministries and churches. And finally, I will share some of my suggestions from my own experience and from others, as well as some of the resources I have found helpful.

The stories that begin most of the chapters are stories I have told during Sunday Celebrations. Monthaven University is a fantasy university located in the heart of the mountains of Virginia in the tiny town of Gateway. The people in these stories struggle with their own faith and how it is to be connected to their everyday lives. I tell these stories to help students see that faith is not just reading your Bible or saying your prayers. Faith is the way we live our lives. Faith guides us as we eat breakfast, or walk to class, or hug a friend, or work in a restaurant. That is how important this business of faith is.

Each chapter starts with a Scripture passage, which shows people who are doubting, people who question or challenge God. The Bible has many such stories, which indicates to me, once again, that doubting is a natural part of the journey. God can handle our doubts.

I am a Christian, a Presbyterian Christian. So this book is written from a Presbyterian perspective. I have tried to include perspectives from other faith traditions since this faith struggle is something that all humans seem to encounter. It is my hope that others will see in it some wisdom pertaining to their own faith tradition, whether that be Christian, Jewish, Muslim, Hindu, or one of the many other forms of religious belief.

Many campus ministers have helped with this project. These are the ones who opened their homes, shared their meals, and spent time in wonderful conversations about their work and mine. I learned something of value from every campus minister. I also saw that every campus ministry has at least one thing it does well. Every campus ministry has some program that is helping students in their struggle toward a mature faith. I did not expect to find that. My own cynicism about the state of campus ministry was greatly reduced. "Thank you" to all those campus ministers who made arrangements for these interviews.

A special word of thanks to those who read rough copies of this book and were kind enough to comment—Lauren Cogswell, Judi Coplen, Amy Edwards, Andrea Sarate, Bill Painter, and John Grace.

Finally, I would like to say a humble thanks to all those students who allowed me the privilege of spending an hour or two listening to their stories. To trust me enough to share the sorrows and the joys of their hearts' journey was a great honor.

1

An End to Childish Ways

Let the little children come to me; do not stop them; for it is to such as these that the kingdom of God belongs. Truly I tell you, whoever does not receive the kingdom of God as a little child will never enter it.

—Mark 10:14, 15

When I was a child, I spoke like a child, I thought like a child, I reasoned like a child; when I became an adult, I put an end to childish ways.

—1 Cor. 13:11

"Why don't you grow up?"

"Stop acting like such a baby!"

"Why can't you act your age?"

Marcy turned the key in the ignition and slowly pushed the gas pedal down. The engine roared to life. She gripped the steering wheel tightly with both hands and looked carefully into the mirrors. Then she gave a nervous look to her right at the police officer who sat in the seat with her. He was an enormous man, probably in his fifties. His dark hair was streaked with gray around the temples. He had a stern look on his face. She wondered how much joy he got from failing sixteen-year-olds who were trying to get their driver's licenses.

"I want you to back the car out into the road course. Go to the stop sign and turn left. Follow the course until you get to the traffic light. Turn right and pull into one of the parking spaces there."

He sounded tired. Marcy wondered how many of these tests he had given today. How many innocent teenagers had fallen on the course so far. Would she find their battered and bloodied bodies lying on the streets of the course? Would she see them staggering back to their parents' cars where they would collapse into the arms of a weeping mom or dad?

As she backed out into the road a surge of panic overcame her. Was she to go to the left or the right? She couldn't remember what he had said. Her view to the right was blocked by a van. She looked to the left and saw no stop sign. She remembered that there was a stop sign . . . somewhere. As she tried to make up her mind, the car went further and further into the road. She looked into her rearview mirror and saw a fence coming up behind her. Without thinking, she stepped on the gas and her car bumped up over the curb and hit the fence post. She slammed her foot on the brake and burst into tears. She had failed! She hadn't even gotten out onto the road!

In her despair she imagined the officer getting out of the car, laughing like a demon. "Hey, Carl! Chalk up another one for me! Yeah, this one didn't even get out of the parking lot! She'll be ninety before she ever gets her license!"

"Marcy . . . " The officer's voice broke into her spinning head. He was calm as he reached over and turned the ignition off. "Marcy, try to calm down. I want you to take a couple of deep breaths. Just relax."

The officer pulled her hands, with some difficulty, from their death grip on the steering wheel. He handed her a handkerchief so she could wipe her eyes. She was afraid to look at him.

The officer spoke softly and gently. "I can remember when I took my driver's test. I had three older sisters. Each of them had gotten their license without any problem. I was terrified. I had heard of folks who took the test year after year and failed. One of my friends at school had taken the test three times. He was in college before he finally got his driver's license. I wondered how I could ever live down failing my test—especially being a guy! I was so nervous.

"When I finally got on the test course, I pulled out of the parking lot without the cop. He was running after me as I went cruising down the course. At the stop sign he caught up. He tried to get in, but the door was locked. As I reached over to unlock it, I let my foot off the brake and the car started rolling forward. I ran over his foot. I slammed on the brakes and stalled the car in the middle of the intersection. When the cop got in, the first thing he said to me was, 'Maybe you ought to come back in six months.'

"I knew I was a good driver. I was just really nervous. I think about that every time I get in the car with a teenager. I know how nervous you are. I want you to relax. Concentrate on what you are doing. Pay attention to everything going on around you, that's what makes a good driver. And breathe. You are going to go to your left, down to the stop sign."

Marcy started the car again. She put it in forward and slowly let off the brake, putting her foot gently on the gas. She took a deep breath as she turned the wheel and headed toward the stop sign. She became aware of the bumps in the road. The yellow lines. Two other drivers waiting to go through the course. As she stopped at the intersection, she looked over at the officer. He smiled at her and motioned with his head that she was to go left.

What Is Faith?

We are tested. From the moment of our birth to the last breath of our life we are being pushed, challenged to move on to the next level. When we take on those challenges we work through whatever issues, whatever problems confront us. We struggle, we fight, we become depressed and anxious. But eventually we come out on the other side, where we look back and see that we have, indeed, grown. When we back away from the challenges, we live our lives in isolation and safety, never being courageous enough to take on the unknown. But also never really living life.

Our physical growth is well documented. It is something we hear about early in elementary school. We look forward to becoming men and women. Our bodies filling out in all the right places. Hair appearing in all the right places. Our voices becoming rich and resonant. But my elementary school teachers and all those filmstrips never told me that puberty is hell. Maybe I was sick that day. But it seemed as though everybody else was caught off guard as well. Suddenly everything was out of control—my voice, my emotions, my body. And what's with all this sex stuff? I was surrounded by beautiful young women whose main purpose in life seemed to be to keep me from figuring out how to diagram a sentence!

Our intellectual growth is carefully programmed. That's what schools are all about—making sure that our brains are progressing at an acceptable pace. There are all sorts of tests to find out just how well we are developing—an alphabet soup of fill-in-the-dots with a number two pencil.

Our emotional growth is a bit trickier. Although parental help books are filled with how little Johnny or Sasha should be behaving by age seven, or thirteen, or eighteen, and teachers are given instruction in preparation for taking on the lives of the community's youngest, there is still a great deal of uncertainty about what emotions actually look like in terms of behavior.

Move into the arena of spiritual growth and we suddenly find ourselves in the barren desert. In fact, many folks don't even think about spiritual *growth*: You are spiritual or you aren't. There is an assumption that faith is connected with adulthood, or perhaps with the joining of a religious organization—confirmation, baptism (as an adult), bar or bat mitzvah, and so forth. One day you don't have it, then you go through a time of preparation, and a ceremony, and then—ta da!—you do have it.

But increasing numbers of studies have led to increasing numbers of theories indicating that we go through spiritual growth—faith development—in much the same way that we go through growth in every other area of human life. Just as a newborn is not without emotions, intellect, or physical aspect, so an infant is not without faith. A newborn's emotions don't look like adult emotions. A newborn's intellect doesn't work the same way as an adult's intellect. A newborn's physical appearance is not the same as an adult's physical appearance. And a newborn's faith is not the same as an adult's faith.

Now you may very well be saying, "Whoa, whoa, whoa! Hold the phone, here, just a second. How can a newborn know about Jesus, or Yahweh, or Buddha, or Allah?" So glad you stopped and asked! The first thing I want to do is to establish a definition of faith. We need something that will cover not only all the different religions, but also no religion—atheism. We need a definition that is going to work even when we have doubts about God's existence—agnosticism. Sharon Parks suggests a definition:

> It is in the activity of finding and being found by meaning that we as modern persons come closest to recognizing our participation in the life of faith. It is this activity of composing and being composed by meaning, then, that I invite the reader to associate with the word *faith*.[1]

Dr. Donald Dawe, one of my theology professors at Union Seminary in Virginia, once said that religion was from humans, faith was from God. We humans are created by God. It seems only natural that God would not wait until we have been through "x" years of religious education to grant us the gift of faith. We have faith from the very beginning. We try to make meaning of things from the moment of our birth. Once again, Parks writes:

> We can only imagine that we come to our first consciousness in a rudimentary sense of dependable pattern, wholeness, and relation—a sense of an ultimate environment that intends our good; we awaken to life as a primal force of promise. Then, in the experience we call birth, we undergo what must seem like utter chaos: sound louder than ever before, light, touch, breathing for the first time. The task of the infant is then the struggle to regain—to compose—that which was promised at the dawn of existence, a felt sense or conviction of trustworthy pattern and relation.[2]

> Therefore the LORD God sent him forth from the Garden of Eden, to till the ground from which he was taken. (Gen. 3:23)

In a way, we each are cast out of the Garden of Eden and thrust into an unfamiliar and hostile world at our birth. But this will not be the last time this metaphor will have meaning. With each new development in our faith life we will find ourselves cast again into unfamiliar territory. We can imagine how Adam and Eve felt as they looked out into the world beyond Eden, because each of us has felt the same way as the world we knew and loved came crashing down around us and we were confronted with new and uncertain possibilities. Kindergarten did it. Puberty did it.

---

1. Sharon Parks, *The Critical Years: Young Adults and the Search for Meaning, Faith, and Commitment* (San Francisco: HarperSanFrancisco, 1991), p. 14.

2. Ibid.

Our first love did it. Our personal encounter with the Holy Other will do it every time.

As we move through the experiences of our life, we see patterns that we then apply to larger, unknown areas of life. We see Mom and Dad in specific roles. We assume that other moms and dads have the same roles. We see that certain foods are served at certain meals and assume that others have those same foods at those meals. We develop ways of getting dressed, taking care of ourselves, socializing with others, and we assume that other people do the same things. We also begin to see and apply patterns of different cultures, different races, different religions. These are all based on our individual experiences and the experiences of those who influence us. We may not have tasted a different food, but we decide we don't like it because Mom doesn't like it. We may not have visited another country, but we decide that we would really like to live there because Dad really wants to live there.

Faith is how we make sense out of these patterns of life. With each new experience our faith changes. We have to take new data and figure out how it fits into the patterns we have already developed. When the data doesn't fit, or *won't* fit, then we have to reexamine our patterns. We may have to change those patterns to fit the data. That is when meaning composes us. We change to accommodate the new experience. It is the "aha!" moment.

The Importance of Faith

Our faith determines the how and the why of everything we do. The meaning we give to things and the meaning that things give back to us is going to form the foundation for all of our actions. How we view our relationships with other humans, with the creation, and with the Transcendent is going to shape and color our work, our play, our education, our loves, and our dreams—in short, all that we are.

The variations of faith actions are as numerous as there are people. An example might be the activity of recycling. I recycle because I believe the Earth is God's garden and humans have been given the responsibility of caring for that garden. I would not trash my own garden, I try not to trash the earth. Someone else may recycle because that person believes God is off doing other things in other parts of the Universe and we need to keep things in order in case God returns. Someone else may recycle because there is no God and this is the only Earth we are going to get and we need to take care of it. Someone else may *not* recycle, because, when the end time comes, we are going to get a whole new Earth and, since the end is imminent, what difference does it make what we do now?

How *we* compose meaning is important, because meaning composes *us.*

Development of Faith

Probably one of the most influential people in the area of theories concerning faith development has been James Fowler. Beginning with his book *Life Maps: Conversations on the Journey of Faith,* Fowler has been exploring the variety of changes that humans go through in relation to the way we make meaning. He has found patterns in those changes—some related to age, others related to events such as going to college, changing careers, or changes in family relationships. He draws on other developmentalists like Jean Piaget, Erik Erikson, and Lawrence Kohlberg to help define and organize his findings, because his stages, especially his early ones, are closely related to psychological and moral development.

Fowler defines six stages of faith development, noting that not all humans go through all six stages. (A significant number of people spend most of their life in stage 3.) He also emphasizes that the goal of life is not to get to stage six. We need to remind ourselves that, unlike many other things in life, this is not a competition. To be at one stage or another is no better or worse than being at another stage. It is just where we are. Many of us are very content at whatever stage we are at. But it is important to define the stages because we will use different images and relationships in our communicating connected with each stage. People also have different needs at each stage. The six stages as Fowler sees them are as follows:[3]

Infancy and Undifferentiated Faith

This is a "pre-stage." It lasts only for a period of eight or nine months during which time the infant develops a sense of trust or mistrust. This is done in relationship with the primary caregiver. Does the person appear when needed, and does the person fulfill the needs? Is the infant fed, changed, comforted, and stimulated?

Stage 1: Intuitive–Projective Faith

Imagination plays a key role in this stage. The child is bringing in all sorts of information and trying to make sense of it. Images and stories of God,

3. Adapted from James W. Fowler, *Stages of Faith: The Psychology of Human Development and the Quest for Meaning* (San Francisco: HarperSanFrancisco, 1981).

angels, heaven, and hell are powerful forces. The child watches carefully as his or her primary adult influences (parents, teachers, ministers, priests, or rabbis) act out their faith. But the child does not know the answers to a lot of questions, and, as a result, he or she fills in the gaps with some very creative fantasies. This use of the imagination is very helpful and important. The images will stay with a person for the rest of their life, continuing to influence their faith. I spoke with many college students who were or were not involved with a congregation primarily because of these very early images!

Stage 2: Mythic–Literal Faith

Hard lines are drawn in this stage. Things are either right or wrong, black or white. There is an equal hardness in responses to one's actions. If the person does one thing, then a particular response is expected to follow. There is an assumption of fairness in responses. Good deeds are rewarded, sins are punished. Everyone is treated the same way. Stories are the primary way a person in this stage will talk about their faith. Everything is taken quite literally. If the story says this is what happened, then the person assumes that is exactly what happened.

Stage 3: Synthetic–Conventional Faith

In this stage, a person's faith must make sense of the many different groups with which the person is involved. Family, the classroom, the playing field, work, religion, and friends may all have different expectations of the person. As a teenager, he or she is able to see himself or herself from another person's perspective for the first time, which causes a great deal of self-consciousness. Traditional authorities (i.e., institutional leaders, parents, etc.) and/or a close circle of friends are the primary source(s) for meaning-making. One's beliefs are based mainly on what the larger group accepts. Faith is not critically analyzed in this stage, but is simply accepted from these outside sources. Not that there isn't a great deal of conversation about meaning; rather it is that the conversation is intended to discover what "the other" thinks or has discovered. This information is then accepted or rejected on the basis of whether or not it fits in with what other "acceptable" authorities have said.

As stated earlier, many people will spend the rest of their lives in stage 3. This is a very comfortable and "communal" stage. As the number of acceptable authorities is decreased, decisions become easier to make. Loyalties are much easier to define—it's "us" versus "them." There is a sense of order in the world and God is always on *our* side.

Stage 4: Individuative–Reflective Faith

This stage is about reflection and the claiming of authority. The reflection involves critical thinking about one's own beliefs. Why do I believe what I do? What or who has influenced those beliefs? How do those beliefs give guidance to my actions, and are those the actions that I really want to take? As a person answers these questions, he or she will develop a belief system that is truly his or her own; but this is, by itself, insufficient. The other piece that must be added to be a true stage 4 is the claiming of one's own authority. No longer are decisions based on what someone "over there" thinks or wants, but now the individual looks inside himself or herself to decide what is right and what is wrong. The outside person or group will, of course, still have an influence, but the individual sifts through the possibilities and is comfortable with the decision that he or she makes, which may be in agreement or disagreement with those outside. "This is what *I* think. This is *my* decision."

Stage 5: Conjunctive Faith

The main theme of this stage is "relinquishing control." In stage 4, the individual is clearly in charge. With Conjunctive Faith there is a recognition that there are many dimensions to truth, many perspectives of reality. Rather than trying to figure which one is right, a person in stage 5 holds the perspectives in a sort of balance. This is not an uncritical acceptance of every idea that is encountered. Along with strongly held beliefs, there is also the recognition that the individual's beliefs are only a partial view of transcendent reality. For instance, a person holds his or her own religious beliefs but also recognizes the *need* for others' religious beliefs to fill out his or her own. As a result there is an openness to new information, allowing it to speak to, shape, and color one's own belief system.

Stage 6: Universalizing Faith

The key word for this stage is "vision." This is not a vision that comes from within; it is, instead, a vision that draws from beyond. It is a transcendent vision holding fast to justice and compassion. It is a vision so strong that persons in stage 6 are willing to give up everything—family, financial security, social status, even life itself—in pursuit of it. This vision of the way human life could be—is meant to be—is so radical that persons of Universalizing Faith may challenge everyone, including close friends and colleagues. They identify powerfully with those who are oppressed and negated and as a result spend their life's energy working on behalf of the powerless to change the world.

Very few people are in stage 6. Jesus would fit in here. Others might include Mahatma Gandhi, Martin Luther King Jr., or Mother Teresa. There are, of course, people in this stage who remain unknown to the majority of the world. But those in stage 6 are going to be having an impact on their communities in some way.

It is important to remember that we cannot move ourselves through these various stages of faith. We can facilitate movement, we can prepare ourselves for movement, but we cannot say, "OK, I'm going to be in stage 4 now." Transition to a new stage depends on a great many factors, including personal experiences and relationships; emotional, social, moral and intellectual development; and an individual's own willingness to walk into the unknown.

The Focus

These descriptions of Fowler's stages of faith are brief and incomplete. Others have described similar stages of faith development. My objective here is not to delineate in detail all the different theories and stages, but rather to paint a picture of faith in motion. Our faith changes as we encounter the world. It is important to remember this as we take a look at the faith of college students, because here, for many, is faith *in transition.*

Most of the students I interviewed appear to be in between Fowler's stage 3 (Synthetic–Conventional) and stage 4 (Individuative–Reflective). Some struggle diligently and intentionally with the tensions, others are more passive. Many students feel alone in this struggle. There is also a sense that this wrestling is not good for their faith. In short, this is a difficult time for college students. Fowler sees this particular transition as being very important:

> The movement from stage 3 to stage 4 Individuative–Reflective faith is particularly critical for it is in this transition that the late adolescent or adult must begin to take seriously the burden of responsibility for his or her own commitments, lifestyle, beliefs and attitudes. Where genuine movement toward stage 4 is underway the person must face certain unavoidable tensions: individuality versus being defined by a group or group membership; subjectivity and the power of one's strongly felt but unexamined feelings versus objectivity and the requirement of critical reflection; self-fulfillment or self-actualization as a primary concern versus service to and being for others; the ques-

tion of being committed to the relative versus struggle with the possibility of an absolute.[4]

Erik Erikson's adult development theory points to *intimacy* as the central emotional crisis of young adulthood. More than simply love, Erikson's intimacy is "a readiness to risk the self in relations of closeness with that which is 'other' or opposite."[5] The young adult now explores the possibility of identity on his or her own terms. Moving outside the need for a group identity, the young adult becomes willing to risk challenging others, pitting his or her own ideas against those of others. Erikson also sees "intimacy as characterizing situations of conflict and struggle, situations of intellectual and spiritual communion, and situations where persons from differing religious or cultural orientations meet and share their traditions' truths deeply and unthreateningly."[6]

This is not any easy task. Where some young adults are able to move into this stage and deal with the many different perspectives offered to them, balancing them, perhaps juggling them, others will withdraw completely or will be drawn back into an overwhelming identity with some particular group. Those who withdraw may become loners on the campus, uninterested in participating in anything, unhappy about everything. Those who are drawn back into the group identity may hide themselves in the beliefs of the group, unwilling to hear other perspectives. The more they are challenged, the deeper they go into the identity of the group, some going so far as to join cults where they are told not only what to do but what to think, even what to believe.

"Transition" Period

Sharon Parks has focused on this "transition" period in her book *The Critical Years.* She sees this time not as a transition but as another stage in faith development. Calling this the "Young Adult" stage, and drawing on theoretician William Perry, Parks relates three strands of development to the faith journey.

The first strand is the form of cognition. Parks identifies the young adult as having "unqualified relativism." This comes about when confronted by competing, yet seemingly equal, perspectives—two or more facts, ideas, or observations that conflict with each other. The

---

4. Ibid, p. 182.

5. James W. Fowler, *Becoming Adult, Becoming Christian: Adult Development and Christian Faith* (SanFrancisco: HarperSan Francisco, 1984), p. 25.

6. Ibid.

young adult is thrown into a sort of chaos and is able to reconcile the differences by saying that there are many truths, all of them equal. There is still not a critical analysis of the competing claims, only an acceptance that there are many claims.

The second strand is the form of Dependence. Referring to the dependence on outside authority that is primary to Fowler's stage 3, Parks sees the young adult as both dependent and counterdependent. By counterdependent she means the "push away from the dock"[7] of authority. Counterdependence pushes against those external authorities of parents, teachers, religious leaders, and others. This involves some dependence, since the dock is still there to be pushed against—a sort of negative identity—but sets the stage for later inner-dependence, which, as opposed to independence or autonomy, represents a willingness to "self-consciously include the self within the arena of authority."[8] Young adults are in the process of developing their own, inner identity but are still under the influence of the authorities from their youth.

The third strand is the form of community. Again referring to Fowler's stage 3, Parks says that youth identify with communities in which they have been present—family, school, religion, and others. With movement into the young adult stage, the form of community becomes diffuse. Young adults experiment with a variety of communities, searching for those that will give them support and nurture in their quest for self-identity. These are, for the most part, temporary, because of unqualified relativism that opens up large numbers of equally inviting choices. The perception that these choices have identical merit makes commitment to any one difficult at best.

The Shipwreck

"I called to the Lord out of my distress,
  and he answered me;
out of the belly of Sheol I cried,
  and you heard my voice.
You cast me into the deep,
  into the heart of the seas,
  and the flood surrounded me;
all your waves and your billows
  passed over me.

7. Parks, *The Critical Years*, p. 55.
8. Ibid., p 57.

Then I said, 'I am driven away from your sight;
    how shall I look again upon your holy temple?'
The waters closed in over me;
    the deep surrounded me;
    weeds were wrapped around my head
    at the roots of the mountains.
I went down to the land
    whose bars closed upon me forever;
yet you brought up my life from the Pit,
    O LORD my God.
As my life was ebbing away,
    I remembered the LORD;
and my prayer came to you,
    into your holy temple.
Those who worship vain idols
    forsake their true loyalty.
But I with the voice of thanksgiving
    will sacrifice to you;
what I have vowed I will pay.
    Deliverance belongs to the LORD!"

—Jonah 2:2–9

The first part of the story of Jonah is familiar to a great many of us. God called Jonah, a prophet, to leave his homeland and go to Nineveh. There God instructed him to cry out against them "for their wickedness has come up before me" (Jonah 1:2). Jonah was not interested in doing that, but we don't find out why until after the whole fish business. Jonah complains that God would simply allow the Ninevites to continue living with no punishment whatsoever after they had repented (4:2).

Jonah really liked the vengeful God. The pattern he saw was a God who would sweep down with flames and earthquakes and destroy those who were disobedient. But after his miraculous rescue from drowning in the sea he encountered a new aspect of God that would not fit his pattern. The disobedient Jonah had, himself, been spared. The vengeful God would have simply destroyed Jonah and moved on. But this God had given Jonah another chance. Jonah was forced to reconsider his perceptions of God and add "mercy" to his pattern.

Jonah's imagery of this changing experience of God is one of a man in the chaos of the churning sea. The image that Sharon Parks suggests to describe the journey toward mature adult faith is a similar one—that of shipwreck. It is, for many, a fitting description of faith in transition.

> To undergo shipwreck is to be threatened in a most total and primary way. Shipwreck is the coming apart of what has served as shelter and protection and has held and carried one where one wanted to go—the collapse of a structure that once promised trustworthiness. Likewise when we undergo the shipwreck of meaning at the level of faith, we feel threatened at the very core of our existence.[9]

As most of us move into our middle to late teens we gain the ability to differentiate ourselves from those around us. We begin to see ourselves as individuals apart from our families, our communities, even our friends. We have been rebelling against the restrictions imposed by our parents since the time we were born, but now this rebellion grows into full force as we come within sight of adulthood and complete "liberation." Gradually all that we have been taught comes into question. We challenge our family structures, our classroom activities, our religious traditions. Everything is up for grabs. The seas are rough and the ship is beginning to fall apart. It is within such a context that our first experience of shipwreck is near at hand.

The shipwreck may come about through any number of events. It may be the death of a family member or a friend. It may be the loss of a relationship, or maybe the move from a familiar place to an unfamiliar place. Perhaps it is a divorce or a parent losing a job. Maybe it's going away to college. Whatever the event, we are suddenly adrift. The foundations on which we had built our lives are swept out from under us. Like Jonah, we are tossed into the chaos of the ocean without so much as a piece of wood to keep us afloat.

■ ■ ■

My parents got a divorce when I was twelve, which was a really traumatic experience for me. I wasn't sure what I was doing, where I was going. I just was, really, very confused and lost. And kind of became really angry. I just kept spiraling, spiraling into a depression. And Catholicism wasn't doing anything for me at all. I started reading a lot of philosophy. And soon after that I started looking into other religions and at Protestantism and seeing what was there. But it just seemed like watered down Catholicism to me. I eventually found Buddhism and started looking into Buddhism and that was something that really seemed to make sense to me. It was something that really seemed to focus the world in the same way that I was seeing it. That the world

9. Ibid., p. 24.

wasn't so segmented, so separated, but it was something that was connected. It was something that was a whole. And I also found a lot of the practices, like meditation and that sort of thing, to be very helpful to me during this time of my life where I didn't feel any sort of security. And being able to just sit down and clear my mind out was really a very helpful tool for me. (20-year-old male, sophomore, Roman Catholic)

■ ■ ■

This student was thrown into the sea by his parents' divorce. He spent many years in spiritual chaos, trying to find some piece of meaning to which he could cling.

There is more to this stage than chaos. Parks suggests also using Richard R. Niebuhr's concepts of "gladness and amazement" to further describe the process.[10]

Gladness comes when one finally reaches the shore. There is a renewed sense of safety, of having at last found the solid ground. One can look back on the experience with a sigh of "Thank God that's over!" There is also a sense of having become something new. We have gained a new perspective, some new knowledge—perhaps wisdom—that we did not have previously and for which we are thankful now.

Amazement is, I am sure, what Jonah felt as the fish spit him up on the shore. Jonah, glad to be on solid ground again, turns around and watches the huge creature swimming back out to sea. He stands with his mouth wide open, his eyes blinking in the bright sun and sees the fish disappear below the surface of the water with a final slap of its tail. Three days earlier he was certain he would not survive. And now here he is, standing wet and sandy on the shoreline. In a similar manner, we can look back on the total chaos caused by death, divorce, moving, or loss of relationship and be amazed that we have, somehow, survived.

> The metaphors of shipwreck, gladness, and amazement point toward the dynamic, transformative character of faith. This is to recover *faith* as a verb, a powerful activity that can be provisionally distinguished from static notions of both religion and belief. Faith is a dynamic, composing, multi-faceted activity. Faith is an active dialogue with promise. The motion of shipwreck, gladness, and amazement describes, not only the primary crises of meaning that punctuates the story of our lives, but also the rocking, flowing, tumbling motion of our every day—as we dwell in a

10. Ibid.

> continual dialectic between fear and trust, hope and hopelessness, power and powerlessness, doubt and confidence, alienation and belonging.[11]

It is unfortunate that so many of our religious communities view faith as something that can be gained or lost, something that we have or don't have. It is a notion deeply ingrained in our religious psyche and reinforced by many mainstream preachers and writers. But one does not lose one's faith because of doubts. Doubts and questions are a part of faith. The shipwrecks (and there will be several) are part of the faith journey. The transition in which most college students find themselves must not be seen as a tangent to that journey requiring conversion or reconversion. Rather, the transition is a most critical part of the journey requiring compassion, understanding, and encouragement.

Marcy passed her driver's test and got her license. The reason she passed was because she had someone sitting beside her who understood what she was going through. This person was patient and compassionate. He was willing to share his own story with her. He gave her encouragement that helped build her self-esteem. The people who are most helpful to us in our own times of testing are those who share these same qualities.

Questions for Reflection

1. When was a time you made a transition (like going to high school, getting a driver's license, going to college)? What did that feel like?
2. Who are some of the people in your life who have been helpful in your transitions? What qualities do these people have?
3. What are some of the things you do because of your faith? What particular beliefs do those activities reflect?
4. What are some of the questions or doubts you have about your faith?
5. Do you think that your religious community views doubt as a part of faith? Why or why not?

---

11. Ibid., p. 26.

2

Trouble in the Church

When the spirit saw [Jesus], immediately it convulsed the boy, and he fell on the ground and rolled about, foaming at the mouth. Jesus asked the father, "How long has this been happening to him?" And he said, "From childhood. It has often cast him into the fire and into the water, to destroy him; but if you are able to do anything, have pity on us and help us." Jesus said to him, "If you are able!—All things can be done for one who believes." Immediately the father of the child cried out, "I believe; help my unbelief!"

—Mark 9:20–24

Sunday morning and the sky so yellow
Blue flashes diamonds out in the meadow
Where the geese flew south but stopped for the night
Winter flew in on an early flight.
Matthew lingers for a moment in the garden.
"Yes, dear Mary, I'll be right inside."
"Joyful, Joyful" squeaks on the organ's tired old pipes.

Well the flowers are dead from a killing frost
That settled one night so all were lost.
Still Matthew's hand touches one crisp petal.
It falls to the ground where the others have settled.
"Mary don't forget we're gonna get a little crazy,
Use the Nicene for a change!
These dried up leaves all break so easy and float away."

Richard Hill, "Matthew and Mary"

The sun pushed its way through a tiny crack between the two heavy curtains and landed silently on the bed next to Brad's sleeping head. He turned over on his pillow so that the intruder lay directly across his eyes. Slowly he became aware of the warmth on his face and the uninvited brightness beneath his eyelids. He opened his eyes, squinting, and quickly buried his head beneath the sheets. But the damage was already done. He was awake.

Brad tried to go back to sleep, but all he could do was toss and turn, never quite able to find that very comfortable position from which he had been so rudely awakened. At last he gave up and, throwing the covers off, he sat upright, his feet touching the cold linoleum floor. He walked over to the curtains and pulled them wide open, allowing the sun to come streaming into his room full force.

"Hey! What are you doing? It's Sunday morning, man. Go back to bed!"

The voice was that of his roommate, Jerry, on the top bunk.

"Sorry," said Brad, pulling the curtains most of the way closed. "I didn't think you were here. I didn't hear you come in last night."

"Unlike *some* roommates, I have a little more concern for the sleeping habits of *my* roommate."

Jerry seemed a little too coherent for having just awakened. Nobody, thought Brad, can put together that sort of comeback fresh out of dreamland.

"You were already awake, anyway. I think I'm gonna go get breakfast."

"What time is it?"

"It's almost nine. What time do they serve breakfast on Sundays?"

"I don't think they do. I think they have something called 'brunch,' whatever that is. But I don't think they start serving till ten."

This was Brad's first week at Monthaven University. All summer long he had looked forward to being on campus, making new friends, taking cool college classes. The first day he was there, he had a sudden anxiety attack. Everything was so different. The buildings, the people, even the mountains looked different. He had grown up in upstate New York, in the small town of Mottville, just outside of Syracuse. But the mountains of Virginia looked unfamiliar to him. A desire to just pack it all back in the car and go home filled him, and all that day he wondered if he had made the right choice.

As the week went by, Brad began feeling better about his situation. His roommate was great. Jerry was from Arlington, Virginia. The two were already making plans for a weekend trip to D.C. so that Jerry could show Brad all the ins and outs of the Capital. Brad's classes were pretty good. Not exactly what he thought college courses would be. The required courses seemed an awful lot like high school. But he enjoyed his first chemistry class and was pretty sure that he would major in chemistry.

Saturday night there was a big party in the gym for all the freshmen. This was not the first of the freshmen activities, but all the others had been sort of lecture style, do-this-and-don't-do-that sort of stuff. And everybody went with the folks on the floor of their residence hall. This feels like kindergarten! thought Brad. All we need is the little rope for everyone to hang on! But Saturday night it was a free-for-all, and Brad could finally meet some of the other fifteen hundred freshmen from other residence halls.

It was shortly after midnight when Brad finally left the gym, his ears ringing from the pounding bass and screaming guitars of the band Born Under a Rock. He stood outside the doors for a few minutes to get himself oriented so that he could figure out which way was the quickest to his dorm. He got lost, however, and ended up taking over an hour to find his dorm, which was right behind the gym.

By the time he got in, it was after one. Oh, well, he thought, at least I don't have to get up in the morning. Brad flopped down on his bed, barely able to get his shoes and socks off before he fell asleep.

If Brad had been at home in Mottville, his mother would have awakened him at eight o'clock on Sunday morning telling him that breakfast would be ready in thirty minutes. Brad would have dragged himself out of bed, and then slowly he'd wake up as the first few drops of water from the shower hit his face. Then he would he'd have pancakes hot off the griddle and maybe some of his uncle's homemade sausage. Then it would have been off to Sunday school, where he would teach the third grade class about Moses or David. Then he would go to church at eleven and try to stay awake while the choir sang and the preacher went on and on about some biblical passage. Then he would walk back home, change his clothes, and the rest of the day was his.

That was at home. Now he was at school.

Brad went down the hall and took a long, hot shower, something he could never do at home. On his way back to the room, Jerry passed him in the hallway with a grunt. When he got to his room he looked at the clock. Nine twenty. He sat down at the desk with his towel wrapped around his waist and considered his options for the morning. He couldn't eat until ten. He could go for a walk. He could go to the library and study. He could stay here and read. He could go to the lounge and watch TV. Maybe play Ping Pong or pool. He looked out the window. The campus was empty. Everybody else seemed to be sleeping in.

Brad was sitting at his desk drumming with his fingers when Jerry walked back in.

"So, what's on tap for a gorgeous Sunday in the mountains of Virginia?" asked Jerry.

"I don't know" answered Brad. "I was just trying to figure that out. I don't think I've ever had a Sunday morning to do whatever I wanted! I'm so glad I don't have to go to church anymore!"

"Yeah, I know about that. Man, I hated listening to those boring sermons and singing all those old hymns. But every Sunday my mom would drag me out of bed and make me go to church with her."

"So, what do you want to do?"

"I don't know . . . there doesn't seem to be much. Nothing's happening until four this afternoon."

"Hmm."

"Yeah."

Jerry stared out the window. Brad stared at the books on his desk. They listened to the hum of the clock and the birds singing outside. Finally, Jerry spoke.

"Well . . . you wanna go to church?"

"No. What would be the point?"

"Oh. I guess I'll just wander down by myself, then."

"See ya!"

Living and Believing—Christian Gnosticism

Americans like to have everything neatly packaged. Walk through the grocery store or the Wal-Mart and you will find every product neatly wrapped in plastic and cardboard to keep it separated from all the other products. This is also the way we live our lives. Each of us is many people. We are sons and daughters, husbands and wives, mothers and fathers. We are students, we are employees, we are team members. We join our different clubs and organizations. But for many of us we are a different person in each of those different settings. There is very little overlap, and often we don't see how one thing connects with another. How does our family life connect with our academic life? How does our employment connect with our class work?

In my first year as a campus minister, I was surprised to see how disconnected the classwork was from what students did outside the classroom. It was all just a bunch of knowledge to be filed away in their brains, maybe to be used later on, maybe not. Then one evening in our fellowship group we were planning a camping trip and one of the students began talking about first aid and how what she had learned in the class could be helpful on this camping trip. It was incredible to see this connection finally being made!

Unfortunately, we have similar disconnections in our religious life. We go to worship, but what we do there and what we say there has little or no bearing on what we do the rest of the week. Brad and Jerry never really knew what going to church was all about. When the opportunity came for not going, Brad seized it, because going to church had nothing to do with the rest of his life. John Fischer calls this a kind of modern Gnosticism. Gnosticism is an ancient philosophy that divides the world into two realms—the spiritual and the physical. The spiritual was what really mattered. The physical didn't make any difference, so you could do anything you wanted. You just had to believe the right things. The beliefs had no connection with the everyday actions.

> The Gnosticism of today is not much different: Believe the right things about God and do as you please. Christians don't actually admit to this as a life philosophy, of course, but it is what many of us do. We have been trained in the nuances of thinking with a split mind.[1]

This "split mind" can be seen in many places in the church. I was a commissioner at the Presbyterian Church (U.S.A.)'s General Assembly (the decision making body for the Presbyterian Church) where a debate about sexual morality took place. A new curriculum was being presented, and part of that curriculum presented what some people thought was a somewhat ambiguous view of premarital sex. During the debate, several of our youth advisory delegates stood up to proclaim their support of total sexual abstinence to the cheers of many of the commissioners and other youth. We had made a statement of belief.

But I wondered how many of those commissioners or youth actually practiced what they were so enthusiastically applauding. How many commissioners and youth advisory delegates have engaged in sexual activity outside the bonds of marriage with no sense of guilt or remorse? If the church preaches abstinence but as members we do what

---

1. John Fischer, *What on Earth Are We Doing? Finding Our Place as Christians in the World* (Ann Arbor, MI: Servant Publications, 1996), p. 19.

we want, what does that say about the relevance of the church? We have become Gnostics.

And sex is not the only issue where this split mind can be found. We have similar difficulty with money, health, and family life. We have two different positions on war, on poverty, on hunger, on ecology. We say what we believe with one hand, but we act very differently with the other. It is little wonder so many youth and young adults are saying that the church has become irrelevant.

Why Do We Go to Church?

> Then Noah built an altar to the Lord, and took of every clean animal and of every clean bird, and offered burnt offerings on the altar. And when the LORD smelled the pleasing odor, the LORD said in his heart, "I will never again curse the ground because of humankind, for the inclination of the human heart is evil from youth; nor will I ever again destroy every living creature as I have done.
>
> As long as the earth endures,
> seed time and harvest, cold and heat,
> summer and winter, day and night,
> shall not cease." (Gen. 8:20–22)

This is one of the earliest mentions of a very basic form of worship. Did Noah make his offering in thankfulness to God for getting him through the great Flood? Or did Noah make his offering in hope that there would not be another? Because these verses are connected to the previous story by the word *then*, we might assume that Noah was thanking God for saving him and these animals from the Flood (interesting that he sacrificed the very animals he had just saved!). From God's response, we might assume the latter. Throughout the Hebrew Scriptures there are instances where men and women worshiped for both reasons—in thankfulness and to seek God's favor. As time moved along and the nation of Israel became more organized and more settled, those times of community worship became increasingly festive and complex. Josiah presented a massive Passover feast after the discovery of the Book of the Covenant (621 B.C.E.).

> No Passover like it had been kept in Israel since the days of the prophet Samuel; none of the kings of Israel had kept such a passover as was kept by Josiah, by the priests and the Levites, by

> all Judah and Israel who were present, and by the inhabitants of Jerusalem. (2 Chron. 35:18)

The early Christians continued to worship in the temple and at home. "Day by day, as they spent much time together in the temple, they broke bread at home and ate their food with glad and generous hearts, praising God and having the goodwill of all the people" (Acts 2:46, 47). The early church institutionalized the Lord's Supper to "proclaim the Lord's death until he comes" (1 Cor. 11:26). It was a remembering—a time to retell the story of who Jesus was and what Jesus had done. Early worship included hymns, lessons, revelations, speaking in tongues, and interpreting (1 Cor. 14:26). It soon became quite chaotic and the apostle Paul had to remind them "God is a God not of disorder but of peace" (1 Cor. 14:33).

Over the centuries, the church became increasingly organized and powerful. It went through splits, unions, schisms, and persecutions. It was responsible for educating millions and also for massacring millions. The church participated in the noblest of deeds and some of the most heinous. There was corruption and there was compassion. Arrogance and humility. In short, everything that we humans are, so was the church. Today we look back on the history of the Church with both embarrassment and astonishment.

So why do we go to church? Is it because it is the "right" thing to do?

I was having a conversation with an older member of a local congregation about how we have to offer something to folks in order to get them to come to worship. He didn't think that made any sense. So I asked him why he went to church. He said he didn't need a reason. He just went. On Sunday mornings that is what you do. You go to church. There's no thought about whether or not you like it or whether or not you get anything from it. You go. That reasoning has existed for centuries. Our culture told us that church is where you belong on Sunday mornings. But society is a little different now.

More and more our culture has been telling us that there are other things to do besides going to church on Sunday mornings. Right after I graduated from college, I went to work in a fabric store. I went in one Monday morning to discover that the assistant manager had been arrested for having the store open on Sunday. That was 1977. There were a set of laws, called blue laws, that kept most stores from being open on Sundays even in a fairly progressive and not terribly religious suburb of Philadelphia only twenty years ago! Those same laws kept stores in some areas from selling beer on Sundays until just a few years ago! But those laws have been disappearing all across the country over the past two decades.

I can also remember, just after I graduated from college, hearing about children having soccer games on Sunday mornings. We had always heard about Sunday morning golfers. But this was children's soccer! And soon there would follow Little League and swim meets—on Sunday mornings! Today the malls are open, many people work, and for some, Sunday is the only day just to relax. There are all sorts of socially acceptable options for Sunday morning besides going to church.

So why do we go to church? Is it because our salvation depends on our church attendance?

God is not a capricious God. The Creator did not set up a whole bunch of rules and regulations just to see who was going to be faithful and who was not. Some of the rules in Exodus, Leviticus, or Deuteronomy were created for a specific time and place. Others were created for all time and all places (deciding which is which is an ongoing controversy in many churches). The same applies to the New Testament. But regardless of which category the rules fall into, their purpose is to help humans live in harmony with one another and with the creation. We do not earn our salvation by going to church any more than we can earn our salvation by doing anything else.

So why do we go to church? Does God need our worship?

God, most certainly, does not need human worship in order to exist or to be active in the world. There is not some sort of power surge sent heavenward by the gathering of believers that will reawaken a god whose batteries have drained over the previous week. In the 1960s there was a great deal of debate over whether or not God was alive—even among pastors and theologians! God has managed to do quite well in spite of the "God is dead" theories and theologies. And God has managed to remain active in the world in spite of boring worship services and sleepy worshipers.

So why do we go to church?

▪ ▪ ▪

I think the purpose of the church is to give a community . . . a community where many voices can be heard. A community where you can find support, and at the same time you're finding support you find criticism. It has the same function in society. It obviously needs to support society, but at the same time it's doing that it needs to criticize society. It needs to tell society it is not doing a good job and that it needs to change. (20-year-old male, sophomore, Roman Catholic)

[The purpose of the Temple is] to facilitate/teach the Jewish faith.

I also think the purpose of the Jewish Temple is to bring the Jewish community together. I've always been taught that we are all one and that's definitely what the Jewish Temple demonstrates. (22-year-old male, senior, Jewish)

■ ■ ■

The church of the late twentieth century is going through an identity crisis. In my years as a campus minister, I have asked all sorts of pastors what they think the purpose of the church is. Most of them have no idea. I have asked older adults the same question. Most of them have no idea. I asked college students, and many of them came up with answers very similar to those above. The key word, heard over and over, was "community."

My sense is that, even though they may not admit it, the older adults come to church for the community it offers. We all go to church for the community. Community is a basic human need. And when folks don't find community in one place, they will seek it in another. Like food, we all have to have it, and we are going to find it someplace or we are going to die. If college students don't find community in the church, they will seek it elsewhere.

Is the church, then, simply another in a long list of social organizations? No, because it offers a special kind of community that is not going to be found elsewhere. It offers a community of faith—a community to help people compose and be composed by meaning. Here is found a community with a vision of how people were intended to live in the world. That vision is painted for us in Genesis through Revelation. Worship, true worship, is a vital part of human life. People of faith join together to support one another on the faith journey. We gather to remind ourselves about who we are, Whose we are, and what we are supposed to be doing. Worship provides us with a framework for making sense of the world and our experiences in it.

But here again is this strange dichotomy of ideas. On the one hand, our creeds, prayers, hymns, and sermons say the church is to be a model of God's vision for humanity so that all of humanity can see how we are to live. Here is where men and women, young and old, different races, different cultures, can sit down together and figure out how we are to act in this world. Here is where we can share shipwreck, gladness, and amazement. Here is where we can care for one another and all of creation. Here is where we can set aside the human constrictions of economic and social class and make certain that basic human needs are met.

On the other hand, our churches tend to be extremely homogenous—one race, one culture, one social or economic class. We are hesitant to give our money, time, or talents because so many other things are so much more important, and we are stretched to our limit. We will split the church over the color of the pew cushions or a name on a window. We build parking decks instead of housing for the homeless. We spend fortunes renovating the church buildings while all around us are neighbors with holes in their roofs and rampant crime on their streets.

▪ ▪ ▪

I get frustrated a lot with the pettiness of some things, some of the debates that go on. . . . I feel like sometimes the church gets kind of hung up on things that aren't as important as people seem to think they are. (19-year-old female, junior, Christian)

No Place for Doubt

> Mystery, wonder, and true worship are largely absent today. Christianity should *start* people thinking; but instead, pragmatic Christianity *stops* people from thinking and encourages them to accept what has already been determined. Instead of engaging in exploratory thought—roaming around in large fields of doubt, paradox, and ambiguity—Christians rush to the elimination of questioning and doubt as the highest truth, and to the effecting of political change in society as the highest good. The idea that one can believe and doubt at the same time is not only unthinkable; it is also viewed as un-American in light of our pragmatic forefathers who saw belief as the opposite of doubt.[2]

▪ ▪ ▪

I would go to a prayer service, like a cantata, you just sing the whole entire service. I'd feel . . . spiritually uplifted. And then, like a day later, I'd just feel like, "Whoa! There's no God in my life right now, I really have to change that!" And it's really scary. And it's still scary, but it's not as bad.

I would love to be a Christian, just like, "Yeah, I'm a Christian!" That would make me so happy to be so super sure. But . . . I'm not. And that's really sad. You know, I feel like I'm alone in that battle. In my church, I feel like there's nobody there to help me. (18-year-old female, freshman, Baptist)

▪ ▪ ▪

2. Ibid., p. 50.

This is not an uncommon story. In almost every student I interviewed I found the same thing. They were told, either directly or indirectly, that the church, the synagogue, or the temple is not a place to doubt. To sit in the belly of the whale and feel that no one around will even listen is, indeed, terrifying. "I believe, help my unbelief!"

After a worship service one Sunday, I spoke with a woman who had graduated from college two years earlier. I told her about my project and my reasons for doing it. She told me how she went to this one church and sat in the pew. She looked around at all the people who were standing up and sitting down and reciting all the words with such great conviction. She felt as though she was the only one who had any doubts. She never went back.

All human beings have doubts about their beliefs. We have questions. We have concerns. The community of faith *must* be a place where these can be expressed. To face some of these doubts in complete isolation is truly frightening. What if there is no God? What if God is out to destroy me? What if I have to earn my salvation? How can I face the world out there? How do I know if I am doing the right thing? These are, occasionally, *life-threatening* questions. And yet, so many times people feel that it is improper to raise these questions within the community of faith. So we are left to ask these questions alone.

I remember attending an ecumenical gathering of college students. One of the sessions allowed all the denominations to gather in separate rooms to discuss "denominational things." In the Presbyterian gathering, the question was asked, "What does it mean to be Presbyterian?" After a number of replies, a young man stood up and said, "Being Presbyterian means I don't have to believe in God!" A look of terror went through the room as folks wondered if any of the press were there and what they might do with that statement.

I spoke afterward with the young man, and I discovered that he did believe in God, but that at times he wasn't sure about his beliefs. He wanted to be someplace where he could have those doubts and be able to talk about them. He wanted to be able not to believe. His comment was, actually, a compliment to the faith community of which he was a part.

Churches do a great many things to discourage doubts, questions, and challenges. Many of the old churches and synagogues have pulpits with thick stone walls raised high above the congregation. The minister or rabbi is protected by an impenetrable and unquestionable fortress. In many congregations people sit in neat, orderly rows facing forward so there can be little or no interaction among the members during the service. Words come to the congregation, but there is no interest in having any words go back except those which have been preprinted in the bulletins. Those words were usually put there by the same person who is also giving the words from the pulpit. So the service is very much a one-way conversation. The congregation's responses are carefully programmed to fit with the acceptable theology. No doubts. No questions. No challenges.

Worship is generally designed by the pastor, rabbi, or priest. If he or she is lucky, a worship committee may help. In the several churches where I have been involved, the worship ends up being designed to suit those who give the most money. There is a consistent concern that if Mrs. Smith or Mr. Jones doesn't like the service, then they will leave the church and take their money with them. This is not a time to explore new theological ideas or to suggest new ways of implementing those ideas in our everyday lives. No doubts. No questions. No challenges.

Sunday school does not do much better. Far too many teachers have no idea about how to answer a young child's very serious questions about strange events in the Bible or descriptions of God's activity. Many teachers get frustrated and simply stop trying, preferring to go on with whatever the curriculum is. But that doesn't help the child and often leaves a negative impression on him or her. Several students whom I interviewed told stories of teachers who just said, "Don't ask any more questions!" No doubts. No questions. No challenges.

Where Is Your Cutting Edge?

"Faith is a journey, not a destination." I don't know who said that, but more people need to hear it. Faith is not static. It is always moving, always changing. It looks different every day. I could go back to the same students I interviewed and ask the same questions the very next day and get fairly different answers. That is true for us all. Our faith is constantly being impacted by the events of our everyday lives. God is continually interacting with us, teaching us, showing us new things.

As a result of that movement, each of us has a "cutting edge" to our faith. This is the place where we have the most serious questions, the place where we are really struggling, searching. For the last few years, my cutting edge has been with the question of other religions and how Jesus can be the "Only Way" and still accommodate other religions. I continue to struggle with it, though I am feeling more and more comfortable with where I am.

Some folks can't talk about their cutting edge—at least not in church. The question may seem trivial to others. Or it may deal with something that is "outside" the theology of the church. For many, the issue of homosexuality is taboo in their church.

■ ■ ■

I was struggling with my sexuality. And that had a major part to play in it because I'd heard all my life that homosexuality was a sin and that God couldn't love me. And that was, like, the big root of my doubt right there. So it completely turned me away from God and my church and things like that. (22-year-old female, senior, Lutheran)

■ ■ ■

There are many other taboo issues as well: premarital sex, alcohol abuse, death. For some the very question of God's existence is not allowed. "How can you be a Christian and not believe in God?" Actually, most of us fit that category several times in our lives. We enter into periods of doubt. The worst thing the church can do is kick us out. But that is what we do with a great many of our youth and young adults who struggle with those questions. We make them feel unwelcome and suggest to them in many indirect ways that "maybe when you've got your beliefs back together again you will be welcomed."

Some don't want to talk about their deepest questions, their cutting edge. They feel it is not right to question the authority of God, or the church. They feel that they have to set a good example for the younger members, especially the children. They must always present a strong faith. Many pastors find themselves in this situation—unable to talk about their own cutting edge for fear of losing their jobs. It is this "cover-up" that has caused so many young adults to leave the church. Like the woman mentioned earlier, we need to know that we are not alone in our doubts. We need to hear from other people who have them and are dealing with them.

Our churches, synagogues, and temples are in a period of major transition. The religious organizations of the twenty-first century will look radically different. Some congregations are already making those changes. They are accepting the challenge of the millennium by opening themselves up to the new things God is doing. They are aware of the changing social and cultural landscape and are ready to adapt their work to fill the needs of future generations. This does not water down or compromise their faith. It strengthens it.

■ ■ ■

Jerry put on his coat and tie and walked off campus toward the closest steeple he could see. As he neared the church, he could see several other students gathered at the door. The sign in front said Gateway United Methodist Church. Jerry was Catholic. He wondered if he should go in. Then, seeing several other freshmen he had met earlier in the week, he walked up the front steps. All of them were hesitant to go in, so they talked quietly outside sharing all the important information like hometowns, majors, and denominational histories. They heard the strains of the organ as it introduced the first hymn, "Joyful, Joyful, We Adore Thee."

"Well, I guess we better go in."

"Yeah, I guess so."

They walked in together, searching for a place where they could all sit. It wasn't hard to find. The church was about half-filled. They sat in the back, ready to make a quick getaway should anything unusual happen.

Questions for Reflection

1. What were some of your early experiences of worship? How did you feel about them?
2. Why do you go to church, synagogue, or temple?
3. What are your spiritual needs right now? How are they being filled?
4. What have been some of your times of doubt? Were those doubts resolved? How?
5. Where is your cutting edge? What are you doing to find some of the answers?
6. What other resources (such as people, books, movies, etc.) have helped you question your faith and/or have helped you find answers to those questions?

3

Where Is the Flock?

"Take care that you do not despise one of these little ones; for, I tell you, in heaven their angels continually see the face of my Father in heaven. What do you think? If a shepherd has a hundred sheep, and one of them has gone astray, does he not leave the ninety-nine on the mountains and go in search of the one that went astray? And if he finds it, truly I tell you, he rejoices over it more than over the ninety-nine that never went astray. So it is not the will of your Father in heaven that one of these little ones should be lost."

—Matt. 18:10–14

This chapter contains excerpts from the interviews with students focusing on their faith histories—how did they get where they are now as far as their religious beliefs go? I have tried to select interviews that show the wide diversity of responses but also show the patterns of faith development. I have not added any commentary, because I want the students to be able to speak for themselves.

■ ■ ■

The summer after my freshman year in high school I was at Amherst College for three weeks and met a lot of people who were very, very different from the people who I had grown up with. And it was kind of shocking at first, you know, people had prepared us to like go out and evangelize to non-Christians and whatever. Actually being in an environment like that I realized that, like, they really didn't prepare us at all for anything and I didn't really know very much about the world. And so, that is when I really started questioning the environment I was in, like, just how sheltered it was. And I got really frustrated for a while in high school with how stifling it was . . . how everything was really force-fed to us. I started questioning a lot. I started raising a lot of hell . . . which got a little funny. But at the same time that also caused me to critically evaluate my faith. And I realized that it really was something that was important to me.

. . . I also have a lot of . . . caution, like . . . I'm not so sure about evangelism . . . more so than when I was in high school. Just by talking to people, how they feel when they're evangelized to. And just trying to figure out what the most important thing to do with my faith is—whether it's service or evangelism, or just living it. That's something I've kind of been struggling with over the past couple of years.

At one point when I was, I think, in high school I was kind of like, well, "we'll leave environmentalism for people who don't believe in Christ," 'cause anybody can advocate for animals, but only Christians can advocate for Christ. I've obviously changed my focus a little bit . . . because I think it is very, very important for Christians to also be very active in service and in environmentalism and feminism.

I guess I get frustrated with the way the church just kind of follows the rest of society . . . kind of kicking and screaming along the way. Like the Christian Reformed Church is just now ordaining women, but if you look at Christ's life, he was advocating women's rights more than anybody else. (19-year-old female, junior, Christian)

■ ■ ■

That month in Czechoslovakia (as part of the play *Peace Child*) was incredible. The people I met, . . . it turned my life around. Before I went I was a very, very shy person. Very uncomfortable. I let my self-doubt rule most of my life. But within the first couple of days I realized that if I didn't figure out a way to come out of my shell, I was going to miss one of the most incredible opportunities in my life, to meet these amazing people. So I did, I came out of my shell. And that began a process of greater openness. And I just learned so much about myself and the way people relate and cultural differences and cultural similarities, about cooperative efforts or the lack thereof. I came back the day before my fifteenth birthday and I just knew that my life was different. And I sort of had this sense of, okay, I've been given an incredible gift and now I have to begin repaying it. And the next day I got a phone call asking me to serve on the presbytery's peacemaking committee.

In a lot of ways it was being involved with the peacemaking in the Presbyterian Church that brought me into a greater awareness of my own faith and my reasons for being involved in the church. And it's probably because that fellowship I found in peacemaking most reflected the fellowship of my earlier years. People would sit down at table together and struggle with questions together and laugh together, and that seemed united.

I really have a lot of questions, a lot to resolve in my own mind, I think. But I also think that my faith is very much fueled by my doubt. But my doubt has never really been overwhelming, and a lot of times I almost hunger for a "conversion" experience because then I feel like I'd be a "real Christian." Cause I always just sort of believed, and I've just sort of come more into my belief as I've gotten older, and I've started to name my belief, and I've found validation, and added dimensions. Like, it's always been there, there's always this kernel within me, and it's just grown, softened and changed. Sometimes that's scary and sometimes that's cool and sometimes it just is. (21-year-old female, senior, Presbyterian)

■ ■ ■

When I was in high school we were talking about Christian mysticism and I asked [the teacher] about it. And she gave me a book of Meister Eckhart. So I went through that and I gave it back to her and I got another one and I read through that. And it was really interesting for me because it was the same sort of idea that I found in Buddhism, and it was present in that Christian concept. And I guess it was then that I started to realize that I could be Catholic and at the same time not agree with a lot of the things that were going on.

I guess it was my junior or senior year (of high school) I started to get really involved in things like Big Brothers and Amnesty International. I spent a week in Appalachia building houses for Habitat for Humanity. At that time I also found a church that was in Cincinnati, a Catholic church. It almost seemed like it had an actual mission to it—the people were happy to be there. There was a lot of music and singing. And when the priest would get up to do his sermon, the sermon wasn't just about how I could feel happy about myself or how I could feel happy about my life, but also about what I could do in my life to try to make the world a better place. (20-year-old male, sophomore, Catholic)

▪ ▪ ▪

As an adult I realize I should have paid more attention (in Hebrew School), and I regret that to this day.

I was immature. I interpreted [that] . . . everyone wanted to convert me. But that was not the case. I'd say one person I ran into here wanted to convert me. But, we went out, had a few beers, and solved that. Basically, what I think has happened [is] . . . I've gotten to know the people and gotten to know their beliefs, and I've learned a lot from them. I think in a college it's really important to learn—not only learn from books but from what your peers tell you and what your professors tell you. I accepted that we're all individuals. If we were all alike, this country would be very, very boring. We all have different faiths, but we all live together and we all have to appreciate each other. (22-year-old male, senior, Jewish)

▪ ▪ ▪

The earliest thought I can remember is being beside my bed when I was a little kid and my mom making me say my prayers on my knees, doing the "Now I lay me . . . ," which I still do.

For thirteen years I went to Catholic school . . . and can tell you I didn't question anything, but I didn't believe anything either. I went and did the first Communion and I did the confirmation and I never had any warm faith feelings, anything like that. I went through the motions, but it was something I had to do.

When I went to college, right away religion was something I was so happy I never had to go to. The Neumann Center kept sending me tons of stuff in the mail. I'm like, "Why? I'm not Catholic." At that time I probably would have said I was more agnostic, you know, and I really wasn't searching, either. That was where I was and I was happy to be right there.

I'd met the Catholic campus minister when I was [on campus] for my interview and I thought she was a really great person and I really connected with her. And I started going to church immediately because I'd heard that she did a lot of the services and everything and I thought that would be really interesting. I looked at it just from the academic sense, like, "Wow, this would be really cool to see this." But I went to church and I felt something, and it was like I felt it for the first time. I came, over the last two years, to really appreciate the Catholic faith because I feel like [the campus minister has] opened up a world for me, not just an academic world, [but] a world that I can feel. I can appreciate the tradition and the roots that I grew up with and at the same time realize that there are changes that can be made in the Catholic Church. So I've been involved in the Call to Actions, going to Detroit to the conferences, finding out what we can do.

I still question. And I think part of me accepting Catholicism again and a relationship with God is that I feel really supported in my questioning, whereas before I went to a really conservative school and so I really wasn't allowed to question. Doubts weren't a good thing then. Now I feel like it makes me stronger. I would by no means say I am really grounded in my faith or anything, because I still have so many questions. (27-year-old female, graduate student, Catholic)

■ ■ ■

I guess probably about my sophomore year (in high school) I really started going [to church] again. We had a really good youth director at that point. He was a really kind and loving man and I'd never found that in a church. People aren't friendly and they don't hang out after church. And it was just really interesting to me to find somebody in the church who was loving and who was interested in me as a person rather than just me as my mom's daughter. And so I started going to youth group and I started getting really involved. And I actually ended up becoming one of the leaders in the youth group. I got really involved and I did a lot of mission projects with my church. It was a lot of fun and I thought it was good because I wanted to help people.

My senior year of high school I went to boarding school. It was an art school and just about everybody there was completely atheistic. So that was really an interesting time. And my faith, just because I always had to defend it—because I'd always get attacked, and they'd say, "Well, how can you say this, you know, where's the proof?" and things like that—I guess my faith jumped a long way in that period because I really had to examine it. I had to look at every aspect of what I believed and ask myself why do I believe this, where is this coming from, what does this mean to me, how do I exhibit this in my life, where do I stand here? And it was really difficult because I had to look at some things I'd never really tried to think about before. I never really thought somebody might debate that.

I was also dealing with some problems, like the ideas of ghosts and spirits which was kind of interesting and it challenged my faith a little bit. I guess I must be really sensitive to "forces," or whatever, but I'd just be walking around campus and I'd be, like, "There's somebody walking next to me—what's going on?" That was kind of interesting because nobody ever talked about that at church. So I was dealing with that on my own. I was like, "Well, what do I do?" And I dealt with that for a couple of years. One of my youth directors gave me all this literature on spiritual warfare and I was like, "OK, whatever . . . " But, I made it through the year without completely giving up my faith. (18-year-old female, freshman, Presbyterian)

■ ■ ■

I do pray every day, but I don't go to the temple. In my house we have pictures of all of our gods and we have a little miniature temple in my house and almost every Hindu does that. And even in my dorm room I have at least one picture of a goddess and then in my backpack I have a picture of a god. And I know, at least once a day, I will say, "Oh please, God, help me make it through this . . . " or, just say anything. So that's why I consider myself a practicing Hindu. Whereas a lot of people probably wouldn't cause, I mean, I do eat meat and I do drink and I do a lot of things that, at least, women shouldn't do. But, that's because of the society.

[Describing a worship service:] There's a tray that goes around . . . and it has a little fire going and when you're singing the song they go like this [motions with her hands] to the gods. I don't know what it's called. It's just one of those things . . . to me, its always been, you just do it. You don't ask why you do it, you just do it.

I wish I knew more about my religion . . . that's one of the things I probably will focus on later. I know, like you said, with college kids religion is always in their background, not right in the foreground. Not always, but for most college kids, at least most of my friends, it's in the background. We talk about it a lot, but we really don't act on it. I don't think about my religion. I think about it when I'm in bed trying to fall asleep or walking . . . to my class. (21-year-old female, senior, Hindu)

■ ■ ■

When I got to be a teenager, maybe it was the whole rebellion thing—you want freedom, you want to get away from your family—maybe it was just me finding myself, but I ended up basically thinking things out. Some of the philosophy they taught in the Christian church, you know, they were agreeable. But some of them I didn't believe. Or didn't quite believe. So I basically started making my own religion for myself. And when I was seventeen I picked up a book on Wicca and I read it.

For two years I played Dungeons and Dragons. Every Friday, sometimes Saturdays. I finally got hooked up to the Internet and found all these people out there. I was, like, "Yes! I belong!" I don't know if it was the aspect of belonging or the fact that I didn't have to hide myself.

A lot of Christians attach a stigma to the role-playing game. It's so Gothic. It's dark. It brings out the more negative aspect of society, of people's desires. But it also brings out some of the positive, too. They take the responsibility of their position very seriously. They try to take care of people. Despite the fact that they have all these negative impulses they follow, they still have very strong attachment to family.

You want to know my basic problem with Christianity? Not Christianity—Christianity's pretty cool. You read the Bible, that's pretty cool. It has a lot of good things to it. The only problem I have with Christianity is, first of all, they read the Old Testament which has nothing to do with Christians and never will because they're not Jewish. And (secondly) they have this weird idea that I could never be as strong in my faith as they are in theirs, and I'm doubting it constantly, cause I really seek God. I think Christianity is a way to control the masses. (18-year-old female, freshman, Celtic Wiccan)

■ ■ ■

After my parents got divorced, my mom lost all faith, and she became an atheist. And then after that she started going back, hard-core, to the old Native ways. She started getting into Nature and the idea of cycles and balance and that's where most of my religion springs from. I don't know if there is a God, but if there is a God, then I love him. I can't prove all this was an accident.

The Wiccan influences—I really appreciate a lot of people in the group for that reason. A lot of my ideas about religion and spirituality come from Nature from the ultimate balance found there.

You'll find a lot of people, in the Camarilla (a vampire role-playing group) in particular, have this real loathing for Christians. I mean, this deep hatred. I don't really feel that way. I feel bad if they get in my face about it, but I feel more like, I really respect that they can be that devout. And religion as a whole in Western society is just totally messed up. It's more of an idea now than anything else. But it is a beautiful thing. It's beautiful that people can recognize their spirituality. Its beautiful that they can go to other places and be spiritual with other people. And no matter how they find their spirituality, I'm glad they have it. Cause I think it makes the world a better place.

Wicca's not a power thing, it's very much a scholarly thing. (18-year-old female, nonstudent, agnostic)

▪ ▪ ▪

I don't go to church here (at college) cause I can't find one I'm comfortable with and that works as hard as my church, cause I'm used to going in and being exhausted at the end of the day. I just can't find that here. But when I do go home, I go straight in and go to work at church.

I could understand what [the preacher] said. The other preachers—I could just hear screaming. That's all I heard, was that they were yelling, and I didn't like it. It was boring. I really didn't understand when they read the Scriptures—I had no clue about what they were talking about. I was probably about nine or ten. No idea of what was going on. But when [the new minister] came in, he was clear, he was exciting.

When we first started (Youth Explosion) we had parents and kids in the same room and [the minister] asked us what we wanted to do. And no one said anything, of course. So he told the parents to get out. And all the parents left the room. And he had a big easel, with the paper, and he said, "OK, what kind of service do you want?" And like a two year old he said, "I don't like to wear a tie." And he wrote down "No ties." And we just went from no ties and no dress shoes and no dresses. They wanted to wear jeans and shorts and T-shirts. And he said, "Do you want your own T-shirts?" And we said, "Yeah! Let's put Youth Explosion on our T-shirts!" And then he talked to the older kids who were like twelve or thirteen or fourteen, and he told us that he wanted us to plan a whole service for one Sunday . . .

We sat down at the table and we planned the entire service. No adults were in the service. We were the choir, the deacons, the ushers, the preachers . . . everything.

The first one was just pretty much our friends, our church, which was pretty big by then, and then they went out and told other people. So every fourth Sunday we would have a Youth Explosion Service. And it kept getting bigger and bigger. And we decided let's have one city-wide. So we went to the convention center and we brought in about two thousand people. And we did it again about two months later and had about

2500 people. And we would have service in parks. We went to Washington to talk to some other youth groups about how they can start this program at their churches. (21-year-old female, senior, Baptist)

■ ■ ■

A lot of times I would consider my family a Sunday Christian family even though we were religious and we prayed before every meal and did prayers at night together. But I still didn't feel as Christian, I guess you could say, unless it was Sunday. It felt empty, even though we had the formality of praying together. I felt like we do it all the time. It's just a habit.

Then we moved when I was about eight or nine. And my sister and my father kind of fell away from going to church. My mom and I went to church at the Baptist church. And we got involved and at that time I felt very into God. I was sure of everything. I knew I was saved, I knew everything.

Last year I had a lot of doubts about where I fell into everything. I kind of strayed away from everything but I still went to church on Sunday. Then I fell back into the pattern of being a Sunday Christian. It bothered me, but I felt that was the only thing I could do at the time.

I'm still struggling, I'm still not sure of my direction. I'm trying really hard, but I'm busy with schoolwork and everything. I feel like I have no time for me. There's no time for God.

I've gone through a whole day without even thinking about God, let alone praying or any of those things I feel I should be doing . . . that I've been brought up doing. And I can't explain why that happens, but it makes me feel like there's no direction in my life sometimes and I feel really frustrated. And then I'll try to pray and I'll get distracted and I'll go on tangents thinking about other things, like what I should be doing right now instead of praying.

My best friend (at home), she's Catholic, we would talk about some aspects of Christianity. And we would both talk about how we weren't sure of what direction we should go in and all this. But here, there's nobody even to talk to about being unsure because they're saying, "Oh, you don't need that!" They're just being a worse influence on me.

Every time I feel I'm farthest away from God or I'm totally unsure about anything religious—when I go to a chapel service there's always something in there that says, you know, "You're still there . . . " and it's kind of strange. But it's nice and comforting. (18-year-old female, freshman, Baptist)

■ ■ ■

The first time I remember being exposed to the church was when I was about three or four years old . . . and my parents took me to my dad's church, which was the Church of Christ. All I remember from that experience was that I really, really didn't like it there. I think one of the reasons why I didn't like it there was because they were always talking about demons and things like that and I never really understood that. It just sort of frightened me as a child. So, that was my first exposure to organized religion.

(After she moved she got involved with a Lutheran church) I started singing in the choir, going to church and Sunday school, things like that. It was a very good environment for me. I learned a lot while I was there and it's still my home church. I played hand bells, I was an acolyte, things like that. And then, I guess, I hit high school and just started having real doubts about my faith. I didn't completely stop going to church but I wasn't going to church as regularly. Then I came to college and I didn't attend church at all.

I was struggling with my sexuality. And that had a major part to play in it because I'd heard all my life that homosexuality was a sin and that God couldn't love me. And that was, like, the big root of my doubt right there. So it completely turned me away from God and my church and things like that.

It made me feel alone and somehow angry because I didn't know why. Because it was like, "I was made this way, it's not my fault; who can I blame?"

One day, one of my friends, about my sophomore year, asked me to come here (to the campus ministry house). And that's when I finally realized that I was just missing something in my life. And I found it here. I found a very welcoming community. It was very loving and supportive. They just cared about who I was and what I was like. (22-year-old female, senior, Lutheran)

▪ ▪ ▪

I never really examined why I was having a Bat Mitzvah. I knew it was kind of what I was supposed to do as a twelve- or thirteen-year-old in the Jewish community.

After that I decided not to continue with the Confirmation classes, which are for the high school students. And I didn't feel like it was important to me. The only real thing I would do is go to Temple on Rosh Hashanah and Yom Kippur and I would fast. Occasionally, I would go on Friday nights for the Sabbath, or Saturday mornings. But it became a really insignificant part of my life. I knew I was Jewish and I never had problems saying I was Jewish, but I didn't identify with a lot of the parts of the religion.

I think one of the hardest problems I had was dealing with the issue of God. I didn't want to outrightly proclaim that I believed in God, but I think that's because I never defined for myself what God was. And I think that's a big thing. If you can't define it for yourself then it's hard to believe in it.

Coming here to college, that's when I noticed a big change. First of all, when I met people who declared I was the only Jew they'd ever met—I had a hard time believing that. And that made me, kind of, look a little more at my religion because I couldn't believe there were people who'd never heard of it or [who] thought it was so rare and uncommon and didn't know anything about it. And then I had an experience with one of my teachers my sophomore year who scheduled a test on Yom Kippur. And I was really upset with that, so I went to see her after class and I told her and she said, "Well, next time just have your priest sign a note and I'll excuse you." And I wanted to say, "Wait a minute! First of all you need to check your terminology because there's no priest. And second of all, I'll be damned if I need to get a note." But I did, I got a note. I felt terrible. I knew no Christian student or anyone would ever have to bring a note explaining why they were missing school on Christmas. I was really upset about that.

I remember things like going to Temple here my freshman year on the high holy days. I really missed my temple at home. And missed the feeling of being there with my family. I'd never missed it before. And when I realized I missed it, it made me think a lot more about it. (21-year-old female, senior, Jewish)

▪ ▪ ▪

Till the age of nine, for two years, I tried to memorize the Koran because there are a lot of Muslims who try to memorize the Koran. At the age of nine my parents had to make a decision under the advice of the religious teacher that either I pursue my academic education in school, whatever, or I do this. And at that time my parents decided that [since] I was the eldest child in the family [and] I was doing very well in academics, that religion should not be separated from the real life. So they decided to take me off the learning process of the Koran. So, I guess it became a big focus in our family to emphasize that, you know, "we are trying to raise you up to face this world as it exists today. But at the same time, don't forget that religion is a part of it. And that's where our aspirations are—that you don't forget religion, you don't think that your family chose that this world is more important than religion."

I had three or four months of deciding before I came here to the U.S., and during that time, I just drilled myself. My parents were more bothered about the logistics—they were more bothered about my financial aid, they were more bothered about my eating habits (I eat kosher meat). They were more bothered about those things, and I was more bothered about how am I going to change.

I see the world slightly differently. I consider myself to be more liberal than other people. I follow my religion but I believe liberally in it. I open my eyes to everything, I try to believe in my religion.

During that time, I think I realized that, no, if I have to be religious [then] I have to do it on my own. I should not be depending on the society and things like that. And I can create a society around myself, not necessarily Muslims, but people who believe that what they believe in is important. And I think, during that time, I did a lot of reading. I think that was the basic point. I did readings from holy texts because I thought I should know that knowledge. And I did readings from people who taught religion in very different ways. For example, I did a lot of Einstein reading. I read religion from a very different perspective altogether. (22-year-old male, senior, Muslim)

▪ ▪ ▪

So I was heavily involved in the Wesley Foundation for a couple of years and more and more found that I was not finding the sense of belonging with God that I wanted to have. The community part was great. But I was really having problems with the nature of Christian authority. A lot of the rules and laws and things laid down biblically are not necessarily applicable to everyone in the whole world. So, although Jehovah God is an aspect of divine, he is not the only game in town, so to speak. And it was really coming home to me that the Bible is to be taken as this ultimate authority, but it is quite self-contradictory in a lot of ways. The only way to accept the Bible as completely authoritative is to just say, "Well, God's trying to confuse me." And so, the more I came to this problem with faith in the Bible, faith in received authority, the less I felt comfortable in a Christian setting.

I went through a thing with the Disciple—where you read through the whole Bible in a period of six months. It's a very intensive, small group kind of thing with the minister and usually four or five students. I was at this place where I was really trying to examine Christianity, looking for a way I could feel powerful in my own right rather than as daughter or wife or sister or even mother. I was struggling so hard to find my own place with my intellect and with my freedom from parents thing, finding a place in life to carve a niche for myself. And a lot of what was going on with Christianity seemed to me to be perpetuating the patterns I was trying so hard to escape from.

So, I sort of spent a year or two casting around looking for something that would be a better answer, so to speak. And I looked into, to some extent, Eastern mysticism, Taoism. Buddhism was too much for me. Hindu—let's sit around and attain Nirvana and exit the world altogether—so that wasn't for me. And someone gave me a copy of a book called *The Spiral Dance*, which is a very good introductory book about paganism in general, Wicca in particular. Its written by a woman named Starhawk. And I looked at the bibliographies and I must have read a million books it seems like. It was really like coming home. It was like, "Wow! Here are people who have words for what I've been feeling for so long!" (25-year-old female, graduate student, pagan)

▪ ▪ ▪

As I've grown up, sometimes I'm forced to go [to the temple] and I don't want to go. And sometimes I'm just, like, "OK, I'll go." Or if I feel like, yeah, maybe I have an exam coming up, or a bunch of exams coming up, and it might be a good idea to spend some time in quiet meditation for my own selfish reasons.

I don't do much [while at college] which is very sad. I do have little mini idols which I keep in my room. I have a little prayer book which I keep in my room. But I do not pray as much as I've been told to. I don't do much. I mean, I do believe I am Hindu and I do believe all the things that I've been taught. Wherever I am I would like to have little idols in my room that symbolize the presence or just to have a link to my religion with me. But, I don't do much.

For me, at least while being here, it's not a very conscious thing—as in I have to pray to a god—it's just my actions or what I think of stuff. I have this theory, a lot of people think it's funny, that I always feel like I'm being watched. Everything that I do, good or bad . . . if it's good, then I'll get something in return because I did it, and if it's bad, then I'll have to pay a price for it at some point in time. So it's not more of a god thing but it's, like, I feel in some ways God is watching me. Many times if I'm waiting to hear about a job or something, I'll do everything good. I'll make sure I do my homework, make sure I study, cause I know that if I don't I might have to pay a price and lose the thing. So, it's kind of a very internal thing. That's my perception of religion, mostly. (21-year-old female, sophomore, Hindu)

▪ ▪ ▪

As I went through my Bible school I started asking questions, and my leader, my Bible school leader, couldn't answer the questions or avoided answering the questions and, like, I felt unsatisfied, so I chose to stop going to church. I guess it started in elementary school. I just always kept asking "Why?" "Why this, why that?" And some people, at that time, didn't understand what the Bible was saying so they couldn't answer me. Therefore, I wasn't interested. I was at a point in my life where I was learning so much, so fast, and I needed answers and they couldn't give me any.

I guess that's where I got interested in Greek mythology. As a young child I loved reading myths and mythologies and was fascinated with, like, the explanations of the world—those were the only answers I had to go on. For example, why does the sun rise and set? The legends gave me my answers. Whether or not the answers were real, I didn't know, but nonetheless they were answers and that's what guided me through my life.

I was always interested in art, but I never followed up on it. I always had the feeling, "Oh, that looks nice, that looks OK, yeah, I like that, I like this." But I never followed up on it to say, "Oh, I'm interested in that, let me read about it, let me learn about it." But now, I'm taking on that attitude. When you see something, you make judgments, and if you don't read about it and find out things about it you always find something wrong with it. But if you read about it and find out more about it, you can say, "I might not like it, but I can appreciate the fact that this person did these steps to produce such an object. And, hey, maybe I've used the same steps to produce a different object that I like. And I can use his steps as well as my steps to create a better object for myself."

Right before I entered high school I heard the word [atheist] and I said, "Sure, yeah, I'm an atheist." Didn't look it up. Didn't know what it was. Then one day somebody told me what it was and I was like, "Yeah, that sounds like me." I might have a stronger religious belief than a true atheist. I do believe in something, I just choose not to call it "God" because when I say I believe in God, people say, "You're a Christian!" Sorry, not a Christian. (21-year-old male, junior, atheist)

■ ■ ■

In my confirmation class, the knowledge was real limited and historical. I remember the person that led it . . . I remember thinking, I think I was about twelve, that he was a sexist and that I really disagreed with him in the things he was saying. I thought he was being close-minded about things and I was having a difficult time with that. When it came time for my confirmation . . . the day of [my confirmation] my grandmother had sent me a cross and another grandmother had sent me a Bible. And I freaked out the morning of the confirmation and I told my mom, "I don't know if I can accept these gifts. You know, a Bible and a cross! I don't really know what that means! I don't know if I even believe in God! I don't know if I believe in it the way these people are teaching me. I don't know if I'm ready to wear this symbol and be, you know, oriented into this religion that I'm not really sure I believe in and I'm not really sure that I support."

Then my mom got very furious and said, "You will get confirmed and you will have your wedding in a church. This is the way it will be!" So I went through the ceremony and that was one of the last times I'd been to church.

In my later teen years, the more and more I heard about the church, mainly, like, Catholicism, and the judgments it was passing, I felt it infringed on my beliefs as a feminist and as one [who is] for equal opportunities for people. The view on homosexuality, I felt, was extremely horrible. As I sort of formed my own ideologies, I was hearing a lot of right-wing conservative people that were basing their arguments from the Bible and pulling things from that. I began to associate religion with being close-minded and with negative things only.

I met one person who changed that for me, who has forced me to think twice, not to judge, to, you know, really be careful about it. And that's a friend of mine. She was a social-work major and we were in all the same activities together. We would talk quite frequently about her orienting her religion and her faith into her feminist beliefs, her feminist practices. That was a big issue for her to try and reconcile the two. Now when I see someone wearing a cross or if someone were to say something about God or something religious, I have to fight the cringe a little bit, but I listen and say, this is just where their beliefs are based. (22-year-old female, senior, unknown)

4

The Cry for Insight

My child, if you accept my words
   and treasure up my commandments within you,
making your ear attentive to wisdom
   and inclining your heart to understanding;
if you indeed cry out for insight,
   and raise your voice for understanding;
if you seek it like silver,
   and search for it as hidden treasures—
then you will understand the fear of the Lord
   and find the knowledge of God.

—Prov. 2:1–5

This chapter contains the responses to specific questions. Again, I have tried to include the wide diversity of thoughts that students have about their faith and its implications for their everyday lives. So many times a student feels as though he or she is the only one who is thinking a particular way. It is helpful to know that others have similar beliefs and are struggling with similar questions.

Who is God?

God is so many different things. Well, the easiest way for me to understand God is as Spirit, though I'm coming to deal more with God in the form of Christ. I definitely understand God in terms of the Trinity. But God the Holy Spirit is always how I've experienced God, a life force that both calms and disturbs and is there flowing through and in and around and above and below everything, from which everything has come and to which everything will return. (21-year-old-female, senior, Presbyterian)

▪ ▪ ▪

I think there is a one, unity, the big cheese—there is no good word for it—the primal thing which is above all, and in all, and the main force. But it's very hard for us humans to sort of conceive of that. It's just way up, it's so hard to touch, that what we do is break it down into images we are familiar with. So, this is not a hierarchy but this is sort of a level of perception kind of deal. So, there's the source and then there's the God and the Goddess—not necessarily representing dualities of gender but sometimes representing spectra of possibilities. And then from there, sometimes we use individual gods and goddesses, pantheons from all over the world, we're very eclectic here. I think the force is the only thing there is, but we can construct whatever image of that we feel like. And so sometimes my best way of interacting with Divinity is to think of that as a person like me. Sometimes the best way of interacting with Divinity is to think of a Mother or Father, or of a dragon, or a rain cloud, or the ocean, or the garden. (25-year-old female, graduate, pagan)

▪ ▪ ▪

An individual who just watches over what you do and how you do it. (22-year-old male, senior, Jewish)

▪ ▪ ▪

I don't think of God as any person or any specific . . . like when I think of God, I don't see Lord Krishna, or I don't see any of the others, or I don't see Jesus Christ. I see something, like, it's the high power that influences my life. It's kind of more like a representation of my own consciousness. But I need to know that, like if I'm going through something difficult there's somebody who can pull me out of it or that if something is happening, it's happening for a reason and that it's all a big plan kind of thing. (21-year-old female, sophomore, Hindu)

▪▪▪

(Reading from his philosophy homework) "God is being. Nothing is not. Nothing is nothing. God is God. Both made of simple parts unperceivably by humans but they are both composites. God is composed of . . . well, if I knew that, I might be famous. Don't know what God is composed of." I don't know who he or she or it is. I do believe that there is a supernatural being that is the head honcho. The Head Honcho. As far as who he, she or it is . . . I don't think it is perceivable by human beings. (21-year-old male, junior, atheist)

Is God active in the world?

A lot of how I know God is through the people around me, and there are moments when that's become very salient, like Peace Child (a touring play), small microcosmic moments throughout high school, some experiences at General Assembly (Presbyterian Church (U.S.A.) national gathering) and definitely lots of my experiences with the intern community (in college). And then random experiences on planes and with people I meet, I just feel that God is very real to me all the time. (21-year-old female, senior, Presbyterian)

▪▪▪

I saw God in those relationships that I developed with those people where I could sit down and I could talk to them. I could be whole with them. And I could be who I actually was with them without any sort of worries about what they were going to think of me or whether they would think that was bad or right or wrong. Without any judgments. Although there were judgments—people were saying, "That doesn't sound like something you should be doing." Or "That doesn't sound like that was really treating the person right." But at the same time they were still accepting you as a person. As a whole person. And not as some evil person who is out doing terrible things. (20-year-old male, sophomore, Catholic)

▪▪▪

I think God is active in you as an individual and then you are in the world. You know, like the world is here and then your religion is your own personal thing. (22-year-old female, senior, Jewish)

▪▪▪

Definitely. God heals people emotionally, and God, I just really feel, is why a lot of people get through their difficulty. (27-year-old female, graduate, Catholic)

■ ■ ■

I don't think that Being is active as far as humans go. I don't think that we can perceive of him or her being active—let me just call God "him" for now—because I don't think that God has time. I think that God sees all, knows all, one big whole picture, similar to Christianity. So, I don't think that I can call him "active." God is not passive, because I do believe that we are a creation of God and if God was passive, then we would not be here. I would say that God is dormant for human beings. Outside of the perception of human beings, I would say that God is very active. (21-year-old male, junior, atheist)

Who is Jesus?

I think that Christ came to show us how to live, not how to die. That's what Christ is to me, that model and that teacher. I still feel like I don't have a relationship with Christ, because for some reason such a concrete God doesn't work for me. (21-year-old female, senior, Presbyterian)

■ ■ ■

From the studying I've done it seems much more realistic to me that Jesus was a prophet and was obviously Jewish, most of his ideas come out of Judaism. One who had an amazing message that I think needs to be told. Trying to break down our limited understanding of laws and structures, trying to let us see that there is something behind and that that is more important. (20-year-old male, sophomore, Catholic)

■ ■ ■

I believe that Jesus is the Son of God, but I don't know what that means. That's what I was taught. I think it's really hard, the whole mystery thing, I struggle with that, but I believe Jesus had great teachings and lived his life in a way that is a role model for all of us. (27-year-old female, graduate, Catholic)

■ ■ ■

I don't think that Jesus always knew what he was doing. I think he was just kind of guided by God, a little more in tune with God than the rest of us because He was part of him. But I think we are all part of God at the same time. Jesus was really special and he was definitely sent by God as an incarnation to help us. But Jesus wasn't completely omnipotent—he didn't know everything. (18-year-old female, freshman, Presbyterian)

■ ■ ■

He is someone who has felt what I feel, been through everything that I've been through. I know that He died for my sins, He came here, He suffered, He upset everything just for me, so that He could die and so that I could go through everything, too. But I always have Him there for me. (21-year-old female, senior, Baptist)

Who is the Holy Spirit?

That part of the Trinity that lives with us—that lives in us. Kind of the part that I don't really understand that well. (19-year-old female, junior, Christian)

■ ■ ■

I have no idea. I'll deal with that one later. (20-year-old male, sophomore, Catholic)

■ ■ ■

I have a hard time distinguishing the Holy Spirit from God. I guess the Holy Spirit can be, perhaps, the wind, or the air, when you're just standing around and you get a brush of something beautiful—I think that is the Holy Spirit. And God is definitely in that and part of that, but I guess the Holy Spirit is just more mobile than God. (18-year-old female, freshman, Presbyterian)

Is there an afterlife?

Yes, I think that we are all part of a cycle. And just like the little pieces of skin that flake off me and are floating around in the air and become their composite elements get used by some other life-form somewhere else, you know a tree falls in the forest and the termites chew it up and the shrubs grow out of it—we are very much like that. I think that spirit and matter are all the same stuff. It's like, when we die we go back to the same pool that we started from. So little pieces of me are all over. I mean, little pieces of me in the tree outside, little pieces of me in Sandy, and in you, and in all of my descendants and all of my ancestors. I don't think there is an afterlife in the sense of this consciousness, this personality, this history goes somewhere else. (25-year-old female, graduate, pagan)

■ ■ ■

I don't know. That's not something I really think about. I don't deal with death very well at all. (27-year-old female, graduate, Catholic)

■ ■ ■

I'm not so sure about the hell end. Hell may be being stuck here on earth or there may be an actual place Hell. I don't know about that. I think that everybody can achieve heaven. I think that probably just about everybody will go there anyway because God loves us and He wouldn't want to see us in eternal pain. I guess if you've committed seriously terrible acts and are really happy about them, you know, and don't feel bad, then maybe you'll go to whatever hell is. (18-year-old female, freshman, Presbyterian)

■ ■ ■

I know I believe in it (reincarnation), but I don't know why. (21-year-old female, senior, Hindu)

■ ■ ■

I think that there's a higher place. I think that when I die I'm going to go somewhere else. I really don't think it will be the same as this great place where I am now. This is just a place where I am and I have to make a difference here and there's a lot of things I need to do to make this better for others and for myself while I'm here. (21-year-old female, senior, Baptist)

■ ■ ■

I think those who believe in a higher being—because there are so many different religions, so many different faiths—I think if you truly believe in this one being that you'll go to heaven. But if you're just kind of "out there" and you really don't believe truly in your heart that there is a God, or your god or Allah or whatever, then you won't go to heaven. (21-year-old female, senior, Baptist)

■ ■ ■

I don't think so. In Hinduism it's very prevalent, like, sometimes you're told, "Don't do this and don't have a bad life, otherwise you will come back as an animal or something." I don't know, I have just never believed it. In Hinduism they always believe that, like, if you get married then you will stay together for the rest of your lives that you have. I just don't see that happening. If somebody presents me with enough evidence to kind of swing [me] you might get me to think about it. But, right now, I don't believe in it. (21-year-old female, sophomore, Hindu)

What is the soul?

A soul is composed of energy, and energy cannot be created or destroyed. Therefore, when the body dies the energy still exists and it has to go somewhere. And I believe the energy will generally go to heaven or whatever you call the place of the dead. I call it heaven because I am a Christian. But I think there are some who get stuck here, or some who are sent here, like guardian angels or some kind of angel being. (18-year-old female, freshman, Presbyterian)

▪▪▪

I guess if you take away everything but your mind and your heart, then that's your soul. The way you feel, the way you do things, you make decisions. (18-year-old female, freshman, Baptist)

▪▪▪

There have been occurrences of people knowing each other from before they'd even met. And they've proven it. That's, like, one of the best examples I can think of for what the human soul has the capability of doing, that is, transcending between lives and people. I would say that the human soul (and this will be a stab in the dark) is in and of itself the key to how humanity continues. We are all part of one huge soul. We all make up the soul. (21-year-old male, junior, atheist)

What is spirituality?

The term is used pretty loosely, as are most terms, but I think it's just kind of being aware that there is more to us than this physical body. (19-year-old female, junior, Christian)

▪▪▪

For me, I think spirituality is a feeling, a concept of knowing that God is with me. The feeling that I have a relationship with God. (27-year-old female, graduate, Catholic)

▪▪▪

I think spirituality would be how you interact with your God, whatever that may be. How you relate to God and how you exhibit that relationship to other people and other parts of your life. Like, I guess for me, spirituality is showing God's love because I'm very big on that aspect of Christianity. (18-year-old female, freshman, Presbyterian)

▪▪▪

It's a process of becoming more human. A process of defining who you are. Becoming closer to that which you believe is sacred. (21-year-old female, senior, Jewish)

■ ■ ■

I think it's being more connected with everything else. Your spirituality is the ability to acknowledge the unseen and the unknown. (20-year-old female, sophomore, undetermined)

■ ■ ■

I think its how you feel your spiritual mind is, like, how conscious you are of God around you. How you use God in your voice and in the things that you do. And I'm sure we all do that, but do we consciously think about it—that's more a spirituality thing. (18-year-old female, freshman, Baptist)

■ ■ ■

A sense of wholeness and a mixture of serenity and excitement. Most times this happens when I connect with really positive things, when I connect with really great people, or there's a tremendous sense of community going on, or it's a wonderful interaction, or I'm in Nature and I'm just struck with how small I am and how big everything else is and how related we are. Sometimes, though, it's even in music. I used to sing quite a bit and play the piano. In singing, the blending of voices with other people, coming together and making this beautiful sound, I feel very spiritual then. I feel very peaceful and very excited. (22-year-old female, senior, undetermined)

How do you nurture your spirituality?

I say my prayers every night and I try to make my days as prayerful and as peaceful as I can. (27-year-old female, graduate, Catholic)

■ ■ ■

Part of it involves having some kind of daily meditation. The point is to be mindful, to put into your life some element which is not necessarily the same every day, but it's a time set aside where you sort of cultivate an awareness of what it is to be sacred. For me, I have a brief meditation and I light a candle and I deal with whatever I feel I haven't liked in myself that day. I look at it hard and try to figure out how I can improve that and then I eat something and drink something. Again, it's the intention, the mindfulness part of doing something with the Goddess/God/Spirit-beyond-all-that-is. . . . Sometimes it's five minutes before I go to class, sometimes it's twenty minutes before I go to bed.

The point is I have at least a few minutes every day. (25-year-old female, graduate, pagan)

■ ■ ■

It [my spirituality] always gets strengthened when I go to church. It always does. It seems like here (at college) I lose it, but I know it's not gone. I just feel like cause I'm not actually in the church setting kind of thing. But when I'm here, I'll pray, I'll read the Bible—which is pretty hard when I've got a lot of other reading to do—but mostly I pray . . . a lot and that keeps my connection between myself and God. Or I'll go somewhere quiet where there's nobody else and just be there—and I know it'll be just me and God cause nobody else is around. (21-year-old female, senior, Baptist)

■ ■ ■

I really haven't done anything. It's more like it's been a part of me growing up, and as I've grown up it's become more conscious for me. Earlier, when I was little, it was very unconscious. I don't even know if I thought about it as much as I do right now. (21-year-old female, sophomore, Hindu)

Are there specific people who have been helpful to you in determining what you believe?

My uncle, who is extremely religious, he's always pressed upon me the Jewish faith. And my younger cousin, who's thirteen, he's very religious. Basically my family has been a really, really big influence. (22-year-old male, senior, Jewish)

■ ■ ■

My dad. I talked to him a lot about my struggles. He has had a lot of the same, even more struggles than I have, and crises in believing where God is and how to make decisions. So, when I am making decisions, I rely heavily on my dad. (27-year-old female, graduate, Catholic)

■ ■ ■

My father has had a big influence. I don't know how to describe my father's religious beliefs, but he was a big trustee in the church, treasurer, deacon, all that stuff. And then he just stopped. Stopped altogether . . . within a three-month period. There was just a big thing in our church about money and people really got caught up. We need to expand, we need to bring more people in, we need to bring in more money, blah, blah, blah, blah. And my father just stopped being a part of that. Last year, we went on a camping trip in the summer—and of course last year I was having a hard time with religion—and we were at a little stream all by ourselves, and we were fishing and just sitting on a rock. And I was fishing and I felt the presence of God, I felt my mind was really clear and that God was there with me and my father. And I noticed that he was praying. And I could tell he really did feel really religious there. (18-year-old female, freshman, Baptist)

How do you determine what is right and what is wrong?

I've tried to set some, like, basic rules for myself, just in an attempt to define things. And I try to take various decisions I have to make and compare them to those rules, so to speak. A lot of it comes from, like, Christ's teachings and what I learned those were. (19-year-old female, junior, Christian)

▪▪▪

A lot of deciding what is right and what is wrong comes from my parents. Like, what I've been taught or what I've learned or what I've experienced. Many times it's not the same as my parents' belief. Sometimes it's also influenced by, like, by me having come here and seeing things differently. Also, I've experienced things apart from home. It's kind of a combination of that. Many times, I can't figure out whether it's right or wrong and I have to kind of go through it to realize if what I did was right or wrong. Everything that I do either good or bad always will come back to me in either a good way or a bad way. So, that's another way I can kind of check if it's right or wrong. (21-year-old female, sophomore, Hindu)

▪▪▪

There's a thing called the Wiccan Rede . . . the idea is with the best of knowledge I don't want to hurt other people. But I don't want to do things merely on the basis of shoulds and shouldn'ts. This is to make me feel guilty for doing something in a certain way. The idea is, Do whatever you want, but do it with awareness of consequences. What you put out you get back multiplied. The Wiccans call it the three-fold law . . . as you sow, you get back three times. (25-year-old female, graduate, pagan)

▪▪▪

Obviously there are laws we have to obey and I utilize those. God does have some influence on that. Basically it's right to go out and help people but its wrong to harm people. (22-year-old male, senior, Jewish)

▪▪▪

With my gut feeling. I always ask God to help me through and I always have this gut feeling if there's something I'm not doing right. I can never tell if it's the right or the wrong thing. But with the gut feeling I know. I know something will happen that day if I get this feeling. And I've learned to listen to it. Before, I was just, like, "Oh, it's nothing." But in the past year I've learned to listen. (21-year-old female, senior, Hindu)

Are some things always right and others always wrong?

I think it's pretty hard to completely draw that line. Like, you look at war and, I'm not really into war either, but at the same time that's been a big part of our history, like, people could say that America wouldn't be a free country if it weren't for the Revolutionary War. Like, the Civil War, I think, was pretty important as far as human rights go . . . so it's hard to say that something is always right or always wrong. (19-year-old female, freshman, Presbyterian)

■■■

I must say, I think that killing is never right. And so if somebody is saying that God is telling them to go kill this person, then I think they are misinterpreting and they're not listening close enough. They're doing it for their own purposes. I think love is always right. Caring is always right. It's always right to help people as much as you can. I guess killing is the only thing that I think is always wrong. Oh, and I guess, probably, like, . . . pollution because, again, that's just completely destroying what God has created and given to us as a gift. (18-year-old female, freshman, Presbyterian)

■■■

I think it seems a little foolish to make absolutes. (20-year-old male, sophomore, Catholic)

■■■

There are some things that you can go into for the right thing and end up doing the wrong thing. Or you can go into something doing the wrong thing and it turns into something right. (21-year-old female, senior, Baptist)

Is there a purpose for humanity?

I haven't found it. (21-year-old male, sophomore, Catholic)

▪▪▪

We are set here, basically, for each other. We need people to talk to, to correspond with. (22-year-old male, senior, Jewish)

▪▪▪

That's another question I struggle with—the meaning of life. I think we are put here for a purpose, but that purpose has not been revealed to me. (27-year-old female, graduate, Catholic)

▪▪▪

What I would consider to be humanity's purpose would be to backtrack and tread this earth a little more lightly and be a little more kind and be a little more sensitive to what's going on and be fair and be just. I don't think humanity's purpose has anything to do with industry or capitalism or imperialism or domination or asserting your superiority over animals or the earth. I think it's none of those things. (22-year-old female, senior, undetermined)

Do you have a purpose?

I like to think so. I don't know just what it is. (19-year-old female, junior, Christian)

▪▪▪

I think my purpose is to find meaning and understanding. Maybe that's everybody's purpose. (21-year-old female, senior, Presbyterian)

▪▪▪

Maybe not a purpose, but a responsibility. I see, like, a lot of things that are wrong in the world and feel like it is my responsibility to try to let people know. I'm not quite sure exactly how to do that at this point. (20-year-old sophomore, Catholic)

▪▪▪

My purpose is to be me. I think my purpose now is just basically to earn a living, to raise a family. (22-year-old male, senior, Jewish)

▪▪▪

It depends on what day you ask me that. I used to think that my purpose was to educate people about different religions. Now I see the gifts I have in helping people through counseling and career development or spiritual counseling. I think that maybe that's my purpose. (27-year-old female, graduate, Catholic)

■ ■ ■

To really love your neighbors and to really give yourself to humanity. I know that I'm here for that. I've known that for years and years and years. (18-year-old female, freshman, Presbyterian)

■ ■ ■

To work as hard as I can to try to change at least one person's life for the better. If it's helping a person to move them out of the Projects or something like that, or to go into a school system and better the education and help get new books. Cause where I'm from there's a lot of problems in the inner city in the schools. So, I think my purpose is to somehow change something, make some kind of difference here. (21-year-old female, senior, Baptist)

What is it that gives you meaning?

My relationships in general, being in relationships with other people, being in relationships where I feel like I'm doing the right thing, I'm out as much, if not more, for their good than I am for mine. I'm trying not to be self-centered. (20-year-old male, sophomore, Catholic)

■ ■ ■

My family, my friends. The biggest factor that gives me meaning is the fact that I strive to succeed, and I do succeed. Success, to me, is the number one factor. (22-year-old male, senior, Jewish)

■ ■ ■

I feel real good when I help people and when I do my best to save the world. (18-year-old female, freshman, Presbyterian)

■ ■ ■

To have a meaningful life, you have to have a certain amount of hard work, you have to have a certain amount of luck, you have to have honesty, and then you have to have faith—some kind of faith. I do believe that you have to have a blend of all those things to have a meaningful life. (21-year-old female, sophomore, Hindu)

■ ■ ■

I'm pursuing this artistic goal. I want to know all that I'm interested in art which includes, of course, different areas, but that right now is pushing me to go along. (21-year-old male, junior, atheist)

■ ■ ■

What do you think the purpose of the church/temple/synagogue is?

It should be a place, a thing, I guess, through which people can learn, where they can come to understand their faith better. I mean, I think that, like, fellowship is very important. To be with other people who believe something somewhat similar to what you do and to really be able to learn from each other. (19-year-old female, junior, Christian)

■ ■ ■

I think the purpose of the church is to give people a safe space to explore and begin to name and to struggle and to find other people to struggle with. (21-year-old female, senior, Presbyterian)

■ ■ ■

The church, I think, is a necessary institution for those who need structure and who need clarity in what they're trying to, like, feel and trying to experience in their lives. They need, you know, a solid structure. They need a church building in order to have someplace to go and say, "OK, I'm here, and now I worship." I think a lot of people would be really confused if they didn't have that. (18-year-old female, freshman, Presbyterian)

■ ■ ■

I don't feel particularly enthralled with the church at this point, at least with the Presbyterian Church. I'm kind of frustrated with it right now because I think it is completely rejecting any doctrines of love. I think the Bible has become something that is used by churches and is used by religion to defend a multitude of things that it was never intended to do and to condemn things it was never intended to condemn. I think they're forgetting the larger doctrines of loving and caring. But I feel that no matter how frustrated I get, I can't leave the church, because how would I ever help it? (18-year-old female, freshman, Presbyterian)

■ ■ ■

To do outreach. Not only to stay within the church walls, 'cause then you're containing all this energy, you're containing everything and you're not going to go anywhere, you're not going to grow as a church or as a person. You're keeping all the good stuff to yourself. I think the purpose of the church is to go and do as many things as you can for the people in the community, to go to places you wouldn't usually go and help out. (21-year-old female, senior, Baptist)

■ ■ ■

I think the church should be a place where people can come together and feel comfortable about talking about God. I would never feel comfortable in my church saying that I don't feel like I'm religiously whole. And I think that's sad because I should be able to share with my church family and say that I do have some problems and I'm sure that there are other people there, I'm sure I'm not the only one that's ever had a doubt. (18-year-old female, freshman, Baptist)

What can the church/temple/synagogue do to be helpful to you where you are right now?

Just by providing a place where people like me can try to figure out, like, what our faith means. The church should be a place where we can get involved in things we think are important like social action, service. I like the fact that I can do Habitat [for Humanity] through the church. (19-year-old female, junior, Christian)

▪ ▪ ▪

Continue to teach me. I'd really, really like to start attending services more, possibly going to an adult education class. Now that I've gone to college, I'd like to go back to worship. (22-year-old male, senior, Jewish)

▪ ▪ ▪

The Catholic Church could provide some sort of token or sign that it understands that society has changed. I don't see the church as having changed at all. Some confirmation that it's okay to believe in change. (27-year-old female, graduate, Catholic)

▪ ▪ ▪

Maybe come here, instead of students actually going to church on Sundays. If there could be something here other than, like, a Bible study, if there could be, like, a service here on campus that would be cool. There is a Presbyterian service that I've been to, but I'm not Presbyterian so it's a little different. I mean, I'll go and I'm cool with it and everything, but it's a little different! (21-year-old female, female, Baptist)

5

What Is "Success"?

When the Pharisees heard that [Jesus] had silenced the Sadducees, they gathered together, and one of them, a lawyer, asked him a question to test him. "Teacher, which commandment in the law is the greatest?" He said to him, 'You shall love the Lord your God with all your heart, and with all your soul, and with all your mind.' This is the greatest and first commandment. And a second is like it: 'You shall love your neighbor as yourself.' On these two commandments hang all the law and the prophets."

—Matt. 22:34–40

I guess I see meaning in my life is by taking what I believe and what I think, like my ideologies, and living them out. And that makes life meaningful to me. Then also by helping other people is a way to find meaning in life. By being connected with other people, by having other people dependent on you and being dependent on other people, it makes everything more meaningful, just because the things I do have consequences not only for myself but also for the people I live with.

—19-year-old female, junior, Christian

Carla sat in the vinyl-covered chair in her adviser's office. She knew the chair quite well and remembered pulling some of the stuffing out of the arms during her sophomore year as she fretted over whether or not that poetry course was going to count to fulfill her graduation requirements. Dr. Evans had spent almost twenty minutes on the phone talking with various folks in various administrative offices trying to figure it out. She sat in the chair and picked nervously at the stuffing.

Carla had come to Monthaven University with high hopes and a rigorous plan for graduating summa cum laude in precisely four years. The university had not made that particularly easy. Each year the requirements for graduating were changed, and students often ended up confused about which requirements they were to follow. Carla was well organized and always made certain that everything was done in the proper manner, but trying to stay on top of all the changes meant regular trips to see Dr. Evans, her adviser for the past two years. Now she was in that worn and familiar chair once again.

Carla was beginning her senior year. As always, she wanted to make sure everything was in order for her graduation in just under nine months. She sat upright and confident in the vinyl chair as Dr. Evans went over her records. Finally he put the folder down.

"Carla," he said pulling off his wire-rimmed glasses, "you've been here three years, but I notice you haven't participated in any clubs or organizations. No sports. No arts. It's all just class work. Is that right?"

"Well, yes! Of course. I want to graduate with the highest honors. I want to have the best grades in the whole class. I want to make sure I have learned as much as I can. I study every night and every morning. When I'm not in class, I'm in the library or in my room. I take this very seriously! I just don't have time for all that other stuff."

"You do have good grades, Carla. Some of the best I've seen."

"That's right! I'm the first one in my family to get to go to college. I worked really hard to get here. My mommy and daddy are really proud of me. And when I show them my grades each semester they know they did the right thing. They made a lot of sacrifices to send me here."

But even as Carla spoke the words, she felt a sadness deep inside. It was a feeling she had experienced many times before—as she watched folks on her floor go out together for pizza, as she walked by herself to class, as she turned down invitations to dances and parties. She always overcame the feeling by reminding herself of what she had to do to make it to her goal. She often chided herself for even wanting to participate in those things. She didn't really care if she had any good friends. She would make friends later. There would be lots of parties after school . . . well, after graduate school.

When Dr. Evans asked her how much time she spent with her friends, she hesitated just long enough for him to know something was not quite as it should be. Her answer deepened his suspicions.

"I spend enough time with them," she said defensively.

Carla then sat in silence. Dr. Evans wasn't sure what to do or say. After a few minutes Carla stood up and walked over to the door. Dr. Evans was about to say, "See you in class," when she closed the door and returned to her seat.

"Can I ask you something?"

Dr. Evans turned in his chair to face her directly. "Of course you can. What's up?"

"Its just, I don't know . . . I work so hard at all this. But I get this feeling that . . . well . . . that I'm still not doing it. You know what I mean?"

"I'm not quite sure . . . "

"I mean, it's like, I got the grades. I know the material. I can do the work. And my parents . . . they just think I'm the greatest. But at times, late at night, I sit alone in my room and I just wonder what it's all about. Is this everything? Is it just about the grades in that folder?"

Dr. Evans leaned back in his chair. He looked intently into Carla's eyes, trying to figure out what was going on with this woman. He saw a look of almost desperation. This was not some superficial sort of a question, it was a question that came from the depths of her soul. It was a question about the meaning of, not just her time at the university, but about life.

What Am I Supposed to Be Doing?

At some point in our lives, each one of us asks the same question. What is the bottom line? It was, perhaps, what the Pharisee was asking Jesus in the Gospel of Matthew. The Pharisees and others had been questioning Jesus, trying to trick him into saying something stupid. Jesus confounded them every time. He looked underneath their questions of intellect and answered their questions of the heart. Oh, yes, the Pharisee and his buddies may have had some sort of trick up their sleeves when they asked Jesus which commandment was the greatest. But there may have been something more to that question on a much deeper level. Jesus may very well have sensed in the Pharisee a sort of frustration with all the rules and regulations, a frustration we all feel at one time or another.

The crisis of faith is, many times, a crisis of the bottom line. We hear people ask, "What am I supposed to be doing?" "What is life all about?" "Is this all there is?" What we have been doing has led us only to this shipwreck, to this state of chaos and anxiety, and we are looking for peace, for calm.

Like the Pharisee in the Gospel, what most of us need is help in loving God and in loving our neighbor. These are the vertical (loving God) and the horizontal (loving neighbor) dimensions of faith. But Jesus slips in a third dimension, which many of us tend to overlook—loving self. The implication is that we can't love our neighbor unless we love ourselves. In Jesus' reply to the Pharisee, we find the components of the mature faith: loving God with all that we are, loving our neighbors, and loving ourselves. When a congregation is helping both its own members and the community in which it exists move in those three directions, then that congregation is being successful in its ministry.

Let's take a look at what mature faith might look like in terms of developmental theory. Based on the work of Erik Erikson, Fowler paints a picture of mature adult faith:

1. This is the adult who has formed and re-formed a strong foundation of basic trust, expressed and grounded in a religious faith or a philosophical confidence that life has meaning. (Loving God with all your heart)

2. This is a person who has a sense of independence, an ability to stand alone, if necessary, on matters of principle. She has clear identity boundaries that make it possible to say a clear no or yes, without undue coldness or distance, on the one hand, or an excessively compliant closeness on the other. (Loving self)

3. The mature adult has a capacity for initiative and purpose, as well as for what existentialists call "having a project." Having a mature conscience, based on examination and considered choice of values and principles, she has reworked the moralistic, harsh conscience of childhood. (Loving God with all your soul)

4. The generative adult has a capacity for work and has developed a set of competencies that equip her to be a productive contributor to society and to carry out effectively the roles and responsibilities these bring. (Loving the neighbor)

5. In the generative person, an adult sense of identity has taken form that can incorporate the range of personal relationships, roles, and aptitudes, as well as limits, into an integrated configuration. This means,

to use Browning's phrase, 'having a personally satisfying and publicly convincing answer to the question, 'Who are you?'" (Loving self)

6. The mature adult has a capacity for intimacy and a readiness based on a firm sense of identity to risk the self in relations of closeness to others, without a paralyzing fear of the loss or compromise of the self. He needs neither to withdraw from situations of intimacy, on the one hand, nor to dominate or destroy that which would get too close, on the other. . . . This capacity for intimacy carries over into readiness to engage in conflict without withdrawal or the need to destroy the opponent, and it sustains one in situations of shared inspiration and creation. (Loving the neighbor)[1]

As young adults develop relationships through campus ministries, congregations, classrooms, employment, and sports, it is helpful for us to remember what a healthy, mature adult faith should look like. We need to keep in mind that all this work is being done over the entire life span of the young adult, which goes well beyond college. These goals are added over the years, beginning from the time of birth and continuing *through* college and, generally, into one's thirties. (The term *young adult* is often applied to those between the ages of 18 and 35.) Young adult ministry cannot stop when a person graduates from college, for the issues of trust, independence, purpose, identity, and intimacy will continue to challenge individuals for many years to come.

We also need to keep in mind that each person moves through these stages at his or her own pace. We cannot and should not try to "hurry" folks along. We can, however, be present to help individuals who seem to be having difficulty in particular areas. Evidence suggests that faith growth is often brought about by a crisis of some sort. I want to use the term *crisis* to mean either a positive or a negative turning point. A crisis could be seen as one going away to college—a positive event—or it could be seen as the death of a parent—a negative event. As we share in both the great joys and the deep sorrows of college students, we need to be aware of how the particular experience may be changing their perceptions of loving God, loving neighbor, and loving self.

---

1. Reprinted and adapted from James W. Fowler, *Becoming Adult, Becoming Christian: Adult Development and Christian Faith* (San Francisco: HarperSanFrancisco, 1984), pp. 26–28.

Loving God

I think of somebody up there just playing with a dollhouse. And there's all these people around there and He can move them around and play with and change all these things, but sometimes He just leaves it alone. Just gotta go away for a while and let it do what it wants. (18-year-old female, freshman, Presbyterian)

▪ ▪ ▪

He's everything to me. Even though it sometimes seems like everybody lets you down, I know that there's God and He's always there. Even though I can't see Him, I can't touch Him, I can't actually sit down and go cool out with him, I know He's there. And it's always a comforting feeling, it's always something comforting me. (21-year-old female, senior, Baptist)

▪ ▪ ▪

These are two very different descriptions of God. In the first, God is like a child who simply plays with the human dolls. God is emotionally distant, detached from the creation, and, at times, walks away to do other things. In the second, God is a very close companion—always present, always warm and reassuring. Other interview responses to the question "Who is God?" were as diverse as the people giving them. The answers came, for most, with great difficulty. There were large pauses as the students tried to find the words that would best describe their experience of and relationship to God.

How can we love God "with all our heart, all our soul, and all our mind" when God is so difficult to define? How can we love God when the line between human and divine activity is so blurred? How can we love God when many times we are uncertain that God even exists? Kathleen Norris, in her book *Amazing Grace*, writes about her struggles with the church and her encounter with the monks at a Benedictine abbey. "I was a bit disappointed—I had thought that my doubts were spectacular obstacles to my faith and was confused but intrigued when an old monk blithely stated that doubt is merely the seed of faith, a sign that faith is alive and ready to grow."[2]

I remember many years ago being in a water safety class in the Boy Scouts. We were talking about how to save a person who was drowning. One of the things the instructor said was that, very often, people drown because they panic. The first thing a rescuer needs to do is to calm the person down, reassure him that he is safe. It may mean that the rescuer will

2. Kathleen Norris, *Amazing Grace: A Vocabulary of Faith* (New York: Riverhead Books, 1998), p. 63.

have to knock him out in order to drag him safely to land. (I am not certain this is an acceptable practice today, but it was, obviously, a powerful image for me back then!) To experience the shipwreck of faith for the first time is, indeed, a terrifying experience. But the wisdom of the old monk holds true—our doubts are a sign of faith that is ready to grow. We cannot allow the panic that is so often the partner of doubt to destroy us.

In our family counseling class in seminary, we were told that when a person has experienced tragedy such as the death of a loved one or the loss of a job, it is helpful for him or her to return to some of the basic routines of life. Cooking, shaving, doing the laundry, or picking up the mail are some of our life rituals that have a calming effect on us in the midst of major upheavals. Our religious rituals can have a similar effect in our spiritual upheavals. Though many of the students I interviewed found church worship services boring and irrelevant, there were a surprising number who continued to attend, especially home churches. This might very well be a response to the chaos of faith. Even though the meaningfulness may be unclear, there is a certain comfort in the pattern, a reassurance in the ritual.

The other side of this lifesaving image is that the rescuer, also, must not panic. Every year at freshmen orientation sessions, I talk with parents who beg me to watch over their children, making sure that they do not get led astray. They want them to keep going to church, to continue the pattern set up in their childhood and youth. I try to reassure the parents that their children may very well stop going to church while in college. They may very well come home with some strange ideas about religion. This is okay. People need to struggle with their faith, and part of that struggle is exploring other ideas and beliefs. Parents can be most helpful by staying in conversation with their children, regardless of where that conversation leads.

Remember the young man who said that being Presbyterian meant not having to believe in God? It would have been easy to jump all over him and pound away with our dogma. But this would have only kept him dependent on an outside authority. Young adults are experimenting with "inner-dependence," the combining of one's own authority with the authority of those outside, and are in need of people who will help them sort through the myriad of beliefs they encounter. They need someone who will jump into the water and swim calmly alongside them as they learn how to navigate the chaos. In this way, the young adult not only will learn how to handle the current shipwreck and find firm footing, but also will be prepared for the next shipwreck.

A conscious loving of God during this transition may not be the easiest thing to do. But God is very aware of this. It is part of our growing relationship with the Creator. The psalms are filled with the anguished cries of doubt and betrayal.

> My God, my God, why have you forsaken me?
> Why are you so far from helping me, from the words of my groaning?
> O my God, I cry by day, but you do not answer;
> and by night, but find no rest.
>
> —Ps. 22:1, 2

> As a deer longs for flowing streams,
> so my soul longs for you, O God.
> My soul thirsts for God.
> for the living God.
> When shall I come and behold
> the face of God?
> My tears have been my food
> day and night,
> while people say to me continually,
> "Where is your God?"
>
> —Ps. 42:1–3

> But I, O LORD, cry out to you;
> in the morning my prayer comes before you.
> O LORD, why do you cast me off?
> Why do you hide your face from me?
> Wretched and close to death from my youth up,
> I suffer your terrors; I am desperate.
> Your wrath has swept over me;
> your dread assaults destroy me.
> They surround me like a flood all day long;
> from all sides they close in on me.
> You have caused friend and neighbor to shun me;
> my companions are in darkness.
>
> —Ps. 88:13–18

Have we failed in our ministries because our college students are unable or unwilling to joyfully sing God's praises? No. We have succeeded in our ministries when we give our college students and young adults space and permission to express the full range of feelings they have in their experience of God. From praise to anger. From thanksgiving to frustration. From trust to doubt.

Loving the Neighbor

The classic story used to define the neighbor is that of the good Samaritan (Luke 10:25–37). Here we find the writer of Luke giving a slightly different setting to the Great Commandment found in Matthew. In Luke the lawyer asks for clarification with regard to "the neighbor" (v. 29) Jesus responds with the story of the Samaritan who shows mercy to the fallen traveler. But at the end, Jesus puts a twist on the story that most of us miss. He asks the lawyer, "Which of these three, do you think, was the neighbor to the man who fell into the hands of the robbers?" (v. 36). The options for defining the neighbor are these: a priest, a Levite, a Samaritan. Contrary to the way many understand this parable, the neighbor is *not* the man who was injured.

We have a tendency to oversimplify the definition of neighbor, resulting in a "band-aid" approach to the problems found on our campuses and in our communities. The Samaritans and Jews were bitter spiritual enemies. The religious dispute had overflowed into their social lives. Jews were not to hang around with Samaritans. They were to have no contact with them whatsoever. And here was Jesus now telling this lawyer that he was to love Samaritans! Look at what Fowler says about a person with mature faith:

> He needs neither to withdraw from situations of intimacy, on the one hand, nor to dominate or destroy that which would get too close, on the other. . . . This capacity for intimacy carries over into readiness to engage in conflict without withdrawal or the need to destroy the opponent, and it sustains one in situations of shared inspiration and creation.[3]

Our campuses and communities are divided in bitter disputes over many issues, including race, culture, sex, alcohol, economics, politics, and education. Loving the neighbor means seeing that person on the other side of the argument as one who also has a desire and a capacity for caring and being helpful. What Fowler is suggesting is that the person of mature faith is able to hold in a balanced tension both her own personal

3. Fowler, *Becoming Adult*, p. 28.

beliefs and a respect for the different beliefs of the other. This is why loving the neighbor and loving the self are so closely connected. To truly love the neighbor, one needs a certain amount of self-confidence in one's own abilities as well as trust that what one wants to do is the right thing. But that inner confidence must be balanced by a confidence that the other person, the person on the other side of the dispute, is capable of participating in the process of helping.

Have we failed in our ministries because our college students still cling to the prejudices of their youth? Have we failed because they see volunteering as just another paragraph on their résumé? No. We have been successful when college students and young adults are able to grapple with a diversity of lifestyles, cultures, traditions, and beliefs. We have been successful when we are able to articulate the tensions we feel in our struggles to accommodate a multiplicity of viewpoints.

Loving Yourself

In the midst of the shipwreck we can get caught up in faulting ourselves for the crisis. We join with others in pointing the finger of blame squarely on ourselves. "I should have prayed more. I should have gone to worship more. If only I had memorized more Scripture. I am weak for doubting. I should have more strength." Young adults are just beginning to trust their own judgments and intuition, so they make easy targets for those who see faith only as an object to be gained or lost.

It is also tempting to think, I don't have what it takes to do this anyway. We have extraordinary models of piety held up to us for our comparison. We encounter people who read their Bibles day and night, who are in constant prayer, whose conversation is peppered with Scripture, and we think, I could never be like that, so I guess I am really not a Christian . . . . or a Jew, or a Muslim, or a Buddhist. We have, once again, judged our faith in terms of an object that is the same for all rather than as a journey with many travelers in many different places.

There is also a certain modesty that many of us have about loving ourselves. We are very self-conscious of our own shortcomings, painfully aware of most of our faults. We do not enjoy the company of those who constantly brag about themselves, and we try not to be that sort of person. When asked to list all the things we like about ourselves, the list is fairly short—some can't think of even one thing! But when asked to list all the things we don't like about ourselves, we can quickly run out of paper.

To love ourselves is to see ourselves as children of God, and, as I saw printed on a poster one time, "God don't make no junk!" We have an appreciation for who we are and the talents we have been given. We see ourselves as men and women of value, not only to our friends and family but also to the larger community. Young adults in general, and college students in particular, are testing out their value. Finally out from under the protective wing of Mom and/or Dad, they can be seen for who they are as individuals. Like a baby bird standing on the edge of the nest preparing for that first leap into the air, most college students are, for the first time, taking responsibility for their lives and for their faith. Like the young bird, the stakes seem frighteningly high.

Loving yourself also means having "clear identity boundaries that make it possible to say a clear no or a clear yes, without undue coldness or distance, on the one hand, or an excessively compliant closeness, on the other."[4] A person of mature adult faith is able to say where he or she stands on a given issue while maintaining a healthy, equitable relationship with those who may agree or disagree. This does not mean holding a forever unchangeable position. It does mean that she will consider opposing ideas and incorporate them into her own belief system as she sees fit. Her ideas may change, but it is because she has weighed the various pros and cons and made a decision. It is not because she felt compelled by the pressure of relationships.

Have we failed in our ministries because college students still have difficulty seeing their own value? Have we failed because they have failed in some of their responsibilities in classrooms, organizations, work, and sports? No. We have succeeded as college students and young adults realize their talents and the value of those talents in numerous situations. We have succeeded when we encourage the "test flight" regardless of the success or failure. I tell my leadership team that all this is "The Great Experiment." There is no such thing as failure, only experiments that need to be done again.

Success in Numbers

Success in the context of campus ministry is often measured in numbers. The more people counted at a meeting, the more successful that campus ministry is seen to be. One of the first questions I am asked when I tell about my ministry is, "How many students do you have?" We are most easily impressed or depressed by numbers. At the Million Man March in Washington, D.C., a few years back, there was considerable debate about the numbers. It was very important for the supporters of the march to have high numbers—the closer to one million the better. It was very

4. Ibid., p. 27.

important for detractors to cite low numbers. The same holds true for our congregations and campus ministries. While most people involved in campus ministry will say that numbers *shouldn't* make any difference, a great many of us have the nagging question in the back of our heads: Why are so few people attending?

So I want to take a quick look at some things that influence how many students will participate in a campus ministry. Some of these issues will be addressed in more detail later.

In his book *The Seven-Day-a-Week Church*, Lyle Schaller says that growing churches will spend $25 to $50 per week per worshiping member.[5] That gives churches some idea of what their budget should look like. Campus ministries should do the same. The question campus ministries need to ask of those who support them financially is, "How many students would you like involved in this ministry?" Then budget, building facilities, and staffing (both volunteer and paid) should be planned to suit those numbers. It is ridiculous to think that one campus minister with no volunteer or paid support staff will be able to minister effectively with hundreds of students. We will look at creative solutions to that problem in the next chapter.

A large percentage of the students I interviewed consider the church to be irrelevant and boring. When they come to college they feel they are, at last, free from the chore of going to church. Rather than offer them something different from what they have escaped, too often we offer more of the same—the same worship, the same Bible studies, the same repetition of meaningless phrases. If churches expect their youth to continue their involvement in college, then some changes are needed in the churches. I will discuss those implications in chapter 7.

Most of our ministries are aimed either at students still in stage 3 or at imaginary students solidly in stage 4. Very little of what we offer is intended to help students whose faith is in transition. That is the purpose of this book. It is my hope that we will begin to offer more programs, resources, and leadership for people who have huge questions about who they are and where they are going. I will discuss some of the programs I think are most helpful in chapter 8.

The bottom line in the "numbers as a measure of success" game is that numbers are important. Huge numbers of students on our campuses are struggling with this transition of faith pretty much on their own. They may feel they are the only ones doing so, or they may not trust

---

5. Lyle E. Schaller, *The Seven-Day-a-Week Church* (Nashville: Abingdon Press, 1992), p. 154.

anyone else to help them. Either way, it is time we took responsibility and made some serious commitments to helping students move through this transition to an adult faith. Most of the major Christian denominations have spent the last two decades cutting back on their commitments to college students. It is time to reverse that.

▪ ▪ ▪

Dr. Evans stretched his arm to the other end of his desk. "Carla," he said as he thumbed through a stack of papers and pulled out a fluorescent pink one, "I want you to go to this tonight." The word *dance* jumped out at Carla.

"Oh, no, Dr. Evans. I don't think I could."

"Why not? It's early in the semester. You don't have any pressing work. I want you to consider this an assignment. I want you to go and meet some new folks. Megan's going. You and she are friends, right?"

"Well, she lives on my floor."

"Great! You and she can go together. Meet some folks. Have a good time."

When Carla got back to the residence hall she saw Megan just unlocking her door. She smiled at her as she put the key in her own lock. She hesitated, then, just as Megan was about to disappear into her room, she very quietly asked, "Are you going to the dance tonight?" hoping that Megan wouldn't hear.

Megan poked her head back out. "What? Did you ask about the dance? I'm going—I wouldn't miss it! Wanna come with me?"

Carla thought for a minute trying to figure some way out, but finally gave in. "Yeah. Yeah, if you don't mind."

"That would be great! I'll knock on your door about nine!"

The dance opened up a whole new world for Carla. She met some great new people and ended up getting involved in the debate team and an aerobics class that week. She was amazed that she still seemed to have time to keep up with her studies. Her hallmates were surprised to find her coming in late one night with a box of pizza under her arm.

Questions for Reflection

1. How do you feel about God? What are some emotions you have felt about God at various times and what caused them?

2. What are some conflicting viewpoints (social, political, or religious) you are aware of on campus? How have the various groups been caricatured?

3. Are you involved in any service or mission projects? Why or why not?

4. What are some of your talents and how do you use them? What do you consider to be your strong points?

5. What has been a crisis point (either a positive or a negative experience) that has opened a door in your theology?

6

Wrestling with God

Jacob was left alone; and a man wrestled with him until daybreak. When the man saw that he did not prevail against Jacob, he struck him on the hip socket; and Jacob's hip was put out of joint as he wrestled with him. Then he said, "Let me go, for the day is breaking." But Jacob said, "I will not let you go, unless you bless me." So he said to him, "What is your name?" And he said, "Jacob." Then the man said, "You shall no longer be called Jacob, but Israel, for you have striven with God and with humans, and have prevailed."

—Gen. 32:24–28

Education has been frustrating and enlightening. But good frustrating in that at least I get closer to the Truth from reading and from learning and from questioning myself and other people. I think that's been one of my big confusing issues—where does Truth come from? Everyone has a different agenda, everyone has a different bias, two people are going to see the exact same event and report it differently. Where is Truth and true representation from people? That's been one of my major problems lately that I think has come about through some education.

—22-year-old female, senior, undecided

The huge kitchen behind Pabulum Hall buzzes, clanks, bangs, whirrs, and spits with activity long before the sun rises. Cooks, delivery people, and student workers all scurry about under the watchful eye of Martha Gibbons, the esteemed director of dining services. Martha has been at Monthaven University for twenty-nine years. She began as one of the servers in the front, working part-time. She had three small children at the time and needed to be home in the mornings to get them off to school. And she needed to be home in the afternoons when they returned.

As Martha's children got older, she was able to spend more and more time working. By the time her oldest was in high school, she found she not only *could* work full-time, but she found she *had* to. She and her husband had to start thinking about college for her son and two daughters. They started putting away some money—a little here, a little there. But they also bought a house, and they needed a second car. So Martha went to work full-time for dining services.

One of the first things Martha did was to extend the mealtimes. Students always seemed to rush through their eating and she felt that a meal was more than simply stuffing food into one's mouth in the hope that it would eventually be distributed to the body as either energy for activities or padding for nonactivities. Most students hoped for the former, but it was clear that the latter was a popular option. For Martha, a meal was a time of nurturing on all sorts of levels. Gathered around the table, friends caught up with one another and families reunited amid hectic schedules. Great ideas were born. Plans were made. Directions were defined. A meal was a spiritual event.

But at Monthaven's Pabulum Hall the tables were filled with the hurried chatter of students caught rushing from class to class. They had only one hour to fill their physical hunger and then—whoosh—the food was picked up and put away. So Martha extended the mealtimes to two-and-a-half hours. Breakfast, lunch, and dinner could now fill up most of a day.

At first, the vice-presidents hemmed and hawed. But suddenly they saw the advantage. They could now schedule noon and dinner-time classes! Well, this wasn't such a bad idea after all! Within a year, Martha's attempt at the leisurely meal had been corrupted. Students were now rushing in at 11:30, gulping down their food, and hurrying off to a 12:04 class on Mondays, Wednesdays, and Fridays, or a 12:11 class on Tuesdays or a 12:08 class on Thursdays. And she would soon have the same problem at dinner!

Even in the midst of the rush, Martha tried very hard to provide a relaxed atmosphere for students. Here were the highs and lows of life, the lights and shadows: the excitement of an entire floor of freshmen men back from a successful water-balloon fight; the thrill of seniors announcing their being accepted at graduate schools or jobs; the joy of couples announcing their engagements; the anger of incompatible roommates; the loneliness of broken hearts; the despair of shattered dreams. It was all here, gathered around the tables. Here private lives became public, and here individuals came to be cared for by the community.

Sometimes the community would eagerly join in with the individual to celebrate a birthday, an engagement, an acceptance. Everyone would cheer, sing, clap, laugh. The electricity of excitement shot through all who entered the room. And sometimes, when the news was dark, when the feelings were low, there was an uneasy, hushed whispering. A person might sit alone for an entire meal, but there was a feeling that others were sharing that one person's particular hurt.

Martha always tried to find time to join in with the celebrations and the mournings. She especially liked to sit and chat with those who sat alone, bringing the comfort of a warm piece of pie along with the love a mother has for a child. She couldn't always do that, and her heart ached when she had to put her job first. These were her tables. This was her ministry. The food she prepared was only a small part. Her employees, the decor, the sights, the smells all added together to make a place that said, "You are welcome here." And most folks appreciated that.

■ ■ ■

How can campus ministries be most helpful to students where they are in their faith journeys? We have seen that the vast majority of college students in the 18- to 22-year-old age range are going through this transition of faith. They may be encountering other truth perspectives for the first time, or they may be grappling with how to integrate new ideas with those they have held most of their lives. They may be very satisfied with their religious beliefs and continue to find them helpful as they sort through the diversity of ideas found on the campus, or they may be unhappy, perhaps angry, with their church, synagogue, or temple. How can we effectively address this wide diversity of spiritual need while maintaining both the integrity and strength of our own beliefs?

I want to suggest three general approaches that can be applied to the various programs campus ministries offer. The first is to provide a safe arena for wrestling with God. This is an open place where students are free to talk about where they are in their faith journey. The second is to provide education. This is more than just a classroom discussion about religion. It entails helping students see what a variety of faiths look like in a variety of settings. It also means helping them understand and take on the challenges of their own faith. The third approach is to provide leadership training. As students become better leaders they will not only be more effective in the work they do on behalf of the ministry, but they will also begin to implement and achieve their own dreams and visions.

Providing the Arena

The best way to have a calming effect on an anxious group is to be curious about how they think about the situation. This is done by asking questions and showing interest.

> Several psychology researchers have discovered quite accidentally that the people they did their research on made dramatic improvements in their personal lives in spite of the fact that the researchers were not intending to provide treatment; they were simply trying to understand the people better. When treatment programs were eventually developed on the basis of the research, those "treated" did not improve as much as the research group. Understanding people is more important than trying to do something to people, to "fix" them in some way.[1]

I was surprised by the large number of students who were eager to talk with me about their faith journeys. I never had to beg anyone to sit down and talk. In fact, as word got around on campus about what I was doing, I had students asking me if they could be interviewed. Many of them were not involved in any campus ministry and had no interest in becoming involved. One of the reasons they wanted to talk to me was because I was committed to listening. I had no agenda. There were no right or wrong answers. I wasn't going to tell them what they needed to believe or how they needed to act out their faith. I was there to listen. And it seemed quite a few of the students really appreciated that.

All of us need places where we can bounce ideas around, but folks who are in these transition periods are especially needful. That is what Martha Gibbons tried to do with her dining hall. Sitting down and trying to put our thoughts into some sort of order so that they are comprehendible to the other person helps us work out the details. It helps us hear out loud what we have been thinking in silence. We can also see and

1. Ronald W. Richardson, "Creating a Healthier Church," as quoted in *Net Results*, May 1998; vol. XIX, no. 5, p. 17.

hear the other's reactions to what we have said. The other can then bring in his or her own perspective to support or challenge us. Like a sculptor, we shape, texture, and color our beliefs as we interact with others who are doing the same.

The arena does not have to be a physical place. It can be an attitude or a concept. We can provide safe arenas for students in the way we talk with them in our offices and on campus. We can provide those arenas in worship services and in service projects. The arena is there for when we honestly seek understanding of the other person. We want to know not only what they believe but what has led them to that belief, what experiences support that belief.

The arena demands a high level of trust. I am grateful that those students whom I interviewed trusted me enough to reveal secrets hidden from all but their closest friends. The trust not only is that what is said in confidence remains in confidence, but also that what is said will not be attacked, belittled, or ridiculed. If we take seriously the shipwreck of faith, we must be ready to hear some pretty strange ideas as students experiment with various blends of religious beliefs. Furthermore, even though these beliefs may be experiments and only temporary, they are, nevertheless, giving meaning to the life of that particular student at that particular time and need to be taken seriously.

The arena is also a place of challenge. We do not simply have to accept whatever is put out on the floor; in fact, we have a responsibility to challenge it. That's what makes the arena an arena. It is part of the wrestling process. We participate in that process by putting our own beliefs out for examination and question. The concept of the arena is there when we live our own faith openly and with integrity so that students can see what our faith looks like and acts like in the real world.

Education and the Challenge to Grow

The fear of the Lord is the beginning of knowledge;
fools despise wisdom and instruction.

—Prov. 1:7

From the beginning the Reformed sponsored learning as a Christian duty. They placed value upon the skills of language, reading, writing, and speaking. They also prized clarity, logic, and precision in mental procedure. They valued the ability to analyze a problem and formulate an answer. The sermon was an intellec-

> tual exercise and a mental discipline that had a significant cultural impact. Yet the Reformed were not intellectualistic. Calvin had warned against curiosity and speculation. The learning that was joined to piety had a strong pragmatic and utilitarian quality.[2]

Education cannot simply be a pouring of facts into an empty mind. To be educated is to develop an ongoing compassionate relationship between the knower, that which is known, and the world in which the two exist. Colleges and universities have the dual responsibilities of teaching students in the classroom and outside the classroom. As campus ministries involved in the life of the campus, we share in that responsibility. We, also, cannot simply pour Bible verses or doctrine into students' heads and expect them to robotically fall in line. Our responsibility is to teach students how to think, how to "analyze a problem and formulate an answer."

We must teach students about their own faith traditions. I was surprised in the interviews by how many students who had grown up in a particular denomination were unaware of that denomination's stands on various issues. I spoke with Presbyterians who were not aware that the Presbyterian Church has policies on the environment, sexuality, nuclear weapons, racial diversity, and inclusive language. There is an assumption that actions taken on a national level will somehow filter down to the youth and children of the local congregation, but that is generally not the case. With so many issues being addressed by the national church, it is difficult if not impossible for the local pastor to make sure that everyone in his or her congregation is aware of every stand the church has taken.

The same holds true for the theologies of our religious traditions. It is very difficult for a child to understand the wording of our various theological statements, but by the time that child has gotten to college he or she should have an easier time grappling with these more complex ideas. Oftentimes students struggle with their religious faith because they have only gotten pieces of the theology. They have heard about the judgment, but they have not heard about grace. They have heard about Paul, but they have not heard about Isaiah. As students begin to question and challenge their religious upbringing, they need to have access to all of the pieces.

Students also need to be educated about other faiths. We live in a

2. John H. Leith, *An Introduction to the Reformed Tradition: A Way of Being the Christian Community* (Atlanta: John Knox Press, 1981), p. 81.

religiously pluralistic society, with not only many denominations in the Christian church but increasing numbers of Jews, Muslims, Buddhists, Baha'is, Hindus, and others. And each of those religions has many different sects with their own variations on the basic theologies. There are some students who come to college never having had a conversation with a person of another faith. There are other students who have a great deal of incorrect information about other faiths. As we compare the differences and commonalities of other faiths, we not only gain a respect for those whose traditions are different from ours, but we also gain insight into our own faith.

The education I am suggesting may be either formal or informal. Classes may be set up or seminars offered. Particular speakers may be brought to address specific topics. Or this may occur in very informal ways during a worship planning meeting, or while on a service project. We must be aware of those "teachable moments" when students are asking questions or encountering new perspectives. It is at these times when theology becomes very real and one begins to see the connections between faith and life.

Leadership Development

> The next day Moses sat as judge for the people, while the people stood around him from morning until evening. When Moses' father-in-law saw all that he was doing for the people, he said, "What is this that you are doing for the people? Why do you sit alone, while all the people stand around you from morning until evening?" Moses said to his father-in-law, "Because the people come to me to inquire of God. When they have a dispute, they come to me and I decide between one person and another, and I make known to them the statutes and instructions of God." Moses' father-in-law said to him, "What you are doing is not good. You will surely wear yourself out, both you and these people with you. For the task is too heavy for you; you cannot do it alone. Now listen to me. I will give you counsel, and God be with you! You should represent the people before God, and you should bring their cases before God; teach them the statutes and instructions and make known to them the way they are to go and the things they are to do. You should also look for able men among all the people, men who fear God, are trustworthy, and hate dishonest gain; set such men over them as officers over

> thousands, hundreds, fifties and tens. Let them sit as judges for the people at all times; let them bring every important case to you, but decide every minor case themselves. So it will be easier for you and they will bear the burden with you. If you do this, and God so commands you, then you will be able to endure, and all these people will go to their home in peace." (Ex. 18:13–23)

Students, like most people, must feel some sense of ownership before they will make a commitment to any group. The more ownership they feel, the higher their commitment will be. I was picking up the mail one day for the campus ministry over in the student center at James Madison University. There is a large, open meeting room where the student organizations' mailboxes are. As I was going through the mail, I overheard bits and pieces of a meeting of some of the students in Student Ambassadors. (Student Ambassadors is a large group of students whose responsibilities include giving campus tours to prospective students and hosting various events such as homecoming and graduation.) This is an organization that is heavily student run. They were talking about fund-raising through their alumnae. It suddenly struck me that here was this large, very popular, very active *student* organization. They had set a mission and goals for themselves, they actively pursued fulfillment of those goals, they were creative in their activities, and they were highly committed to the organization. Why couldn't our campus ministry be like that?

I looked at several of the campus ministries at JMU that are growing with highly committed students. I saw that the campus ministers had stepped back from being involved in every single activity of the students and instead allowed the students to make decisions about what would be done and how it would done. Our ministry, on the other hand, was one in which the campus minister was expected to "micromanage" everything. I was expected to be involved in every single activity, to be present at every meeting, to control every program. As I let go of that responsibility, our ministry began to grow. As I trusted the students to make good decisions, we had more students being involved.

But there is more to garnering commitments from students than simply having the campus minister step aside. There must be a strong and compelling vision for the ministry—a reason for its existence now and a reason for it to continue into the future. Unfortunately, the same uncertainty about purpose found in our churches is also found in our campus ministries. We are most attracted to organizations that have a vision that is clear, concise, and fills the needs we feel are important.

Campus ministries must ask that very difficult question, "What is our role on this campus?"

Campus ministry is today where the church will be in twenty years. It is not hard to see a strong relationship between what is happening on our campuses and what goes on in the rest of society. Colleges and universities are supposed to be ahead of everyone else. The work done in the classrooms and laboratories paves the way for the future. Why should this not be just as true for our religious institutions? As the parachurch groups have grown in strength on our campuses, so have nondenominational churches, a generation later, grown in our communities. As funding for campus ministries has dwindled, so has funding for our churches, a generation later. As the importance of denominationalism has declined on the campus, so has that importance declined in our communities, once again, a generation later.

We can look at these patterns in despair and see the very difficult road that lies ahead for our churches, or we can look at these patterns in hopefulness as campus ministries are gaining a new vitality. If we are truly interested in revitalizing our churches then we must begin with campus ministries. If we are interested in integrating our churches, then we must integrate our campus ministries. If we want our churches to be actively involved in solving the problems of the community, then we must get our campus ministries actively involved in our communities. But to do all these things requires leadership.

It is not enough for campus ministers to step back. It is not enough to write a vision statement, no matter how compelling it might be. We must teach people how to move from the vision to action, how to take the idea and make it actually happen. All too often our committee meetings end up being exercises in frustration because we can't go from *talking* about doing to actually *doing*. If our ministries are going to have a positive impact on the larger campus, then we must train our students to be good leaders.

But good leadership goes far beyond the campus ministry. Students are involved in other organizations on the campus and off. They work with one another on class projects. They work in various businesses. And after graduation, students will be involved in businesses, they will serve on nonprofit boards, and they will serve in local congregations. To develop good leadership skills will not only enhance a person's self-esteem, but will also better enable that person to serve his or her community now and in the future.

With a renewed interest in leadership development coming from the business world, sparked by books such as Stephen Covey's *Seven Habits of Highly Effective People* (New York: Simon & Schuster, 1989) and Peter M. Senge's *The Fifth Discipline* (New York: Currency/Doubleday, 1990) many campuses are now offering leadership training workshops and classes. These provide good places for students and campus ministry leaders to work on their own leadership skills. Because of a reluctance on the part of many state schools to address the spiritual issues involved in leadership, students will need to turn to campus ministries to fill that gap. Many of the popular leadership development books and manuals do, however, address the spiritual dimension. Also a number of resources coming from religious organizations look at leadership through the eyes of faith.

Once again, leadership development can be done informally as well as formally. I meet with our student president once a week to discuss her leadership style, to talk about her vision for the group, and to just check in with her and make sure she's doing all right. But I have much less formal, though similar conversations, with other members of the leadership team. Wherever students are in charge of programs and events, they are developing their leadership skills. It is up to campus ministry leaders to be aware of those teachable moments where we can offer a suggestion, a word of encouragement, or some helpful criticism.

Student Ministries

There are almost fifteen thousand students at James Madison University. We are not among the largest universities in the United States, but we are, still, a good sized campus. On this campus there are about twenty-five officially recognized campus ministries representing all the major Christian denominations, several of the parachurch groups (like Intervarsity, Campus Crusade for Christ, and Fellowship of Christian Athletes), and several non-Christian groups including Hillel (Jewish), the Muslim Student Association, and a Baha'i group. Most of the groups have a staff person, but only a few have a full-time minister or director. The idea that this handful of people will be able to assist fifteen thousand students in their various faith crises is ridiculous. Yet many in our congregations expect exactly that.

Several decades ago a model of ministry called "The Ministry of Presence" was popularized, and it is still in place on many campuses. This model was based on the notion that if a minister was simply placed on (or near) the campus, then students who were in need would seek that person out. Ministers were then responsible for only those students who walked through their doors. This made a campus minister's job far more realistic, as he or she could work closely with a small group of students without being overwhelmed. But, as monetary resources of local congregations began dwindling, the people in those congregations looked with increasing skepticism at the cost of campus ministry in relation to the numbers of students involved. The idea that sufficient numbers of students would be seeking out a campus minister to justify the cost of a full-time staff and physical facilities was also ridiculous.

Both the above ideas are based on serious misconceptions. In the first, there is the misconception that a minister, priest, or rabbi does everything. Only in a dying congregation is that true. In healthy congregations there is a high level of volunteer support and commitment. Worship leaders, teachers, choir members, nursery attendants, grounds keepers, painters, and many others all come from the members of the congregation who have made various degrees of commitment to the vision of that church, synagogue, or temple. They all help to do the work and, as a result, multiply the leader's effectiveness many times.

The second idea is based on the misconception that students will turn to a religious organization in times of trouble. As we have seen from the research and from the interviews, religious institutions are often the last places students will turn to. Students will turn to other students, faculty, or staff. They will get drunk or get high. They will turn to violence. Many students turn to some sort of counseling service provided by the college or university that is, generally, running at full capacity. Or they will try to take care of things by themselves. The vast majority of students will not turn to a campus minister.

But both these ideas also have something to offer when thinking about an effective model for campus ministry. Campus ministers do need to think of their ministry in terms of the entire campus, whether that be five hundred students or fifty thousand. Almost every student on campus is struggling with this crisis of faith. We do have a responsibility for every one of them! At the same time, I cannot be involved individually and intensely with more than a dozen, maybe twenty students, and expect to keep my sanity. My presence must empower others to be present in other places.

I constantly remind students involved in our campus ministry that each one of them is called to a ministry right here and right now. God may very well be preparing them for a future ministry, but there is one, maybe several, to which they are called today. That may be a ministry to a roommate or a teammate. It may be a ministry in the classroom or in the workplace. It may be a ministry in the campus community or in the larger community. Somewhere each one of us is called to do justice, love kindness, and demonstrate humility in our faith. Somehow each one of us is called to love our neighbor, each one of us is called to help a neighbor love himself or herself, each one of us is called to help another explore his or her relationship with God.

My job as a campus minister is to help students discover these ministries and then to be a resource for them—empowering them, encouraging them, teaching them. I do not have to generate programs for them. Instead, I try to discover where they are being called, then find others with similar calls and gather them together. Our most successful programs are, consistently, those programs created by students. When students are passionate about the work, when they feel a real "soulful" connection, then they are eager to tell others, they are more than willing to spend extra time and energy, and they are interested in overcoming the obstacles.

When students are empowered to do ministry, it can cause a ripple effect on campus. As the campus minister empowers his or her handful of students to seek justice, love kindness, and walk humbly with God, those students spread out to the far corners of the campus and encourage others to do the same. Then those spread out and the ripple continues. In this way, even a small campus ministry can have a large effect on the campus, though that effect may be quite difficult to measure!

This sounds so simple. Why doesn't this happen? It is because the same thing happens in our campus ministries that has been happening in our congregations. Faith is seen as something that you tend to one day a week and the rest of the time it doesn't matter. Too often we do not make a connection between our faith and the realities of everyday life on campus. What does justice look like in the classroom, residence hall, playing field, or dining hall? What does kindness look like in relationships with classmates, friends, Greek brothers and sisters, boyfriends and girlfriends? What does a humble walk with God look like in our encounters with people of differing faiths, cultures, or traditions? When we come out of the theological ozone and help students grapple with these questions of everyday realities, then we begin to empower them to help other students do the same.

The purpose of campus ministry is the nurture and faith development of students. It sounds so easy. It is so important. How we make meaning out of life's experiences forms the foundation for everything we do. We need to start taking that a little more seriously. To be present in the midst of this crisis of faith, to be "in the water" with students as they learn to cope with the tragedies, the conflicts, and the challenges is a high calling, indeed. To work with students as they begin to claim their faith, as they learn to trust the water, as they find the land is one of the greatest honors I have known.

Questions for Discussion

1. Where are your "arenas" for discussing important issues? What makes them safe?
2. As you have questioned your faith, what are some of the things you have learned? Who are some of the people who have been most helpful?
3. What have you learned about other faiths? If you have had conversations with people of other faiths, what did you learn from them? What are some of the similarities between your faith and theirs? What are some of the differences?
4. In what ways do you exercise your own leadership? What are some of your best leadership qualities? Which ones do you need to work on?
5. Who are some good leaders on campus? What makes them good leaders?
6. What is one of the ministries to which you feel called? What gifts do you have that enable you to do that ministry? What knowledge or skills do you need to help you do that ministry better?
7. What is an area of need on campus? What could a campus ministry do to help fill that need?

7

"*I AM* Has Sent Me to You"

"The cry of the Israelites has now come to me; I have also seen how the Egyptians oppress them. So come, I will send you to Pharaoh to bring my people, the Israelites, out of Egypt." But Moses said to God, "Who am I that I should go to Pharaoh, and bring the Israelites out of Egypt?" He said, "I will be with you; and this shall be a sign for you that it is I who sent you: when you have brought the people out of Egypt, you shall worship God on this mountain."

But Moses said to God, "If I come to the Israelites and say to them, 'The God of your ancestors has sent me to you,' and they ask me, 'What is his name?' what shall I say to them?" God said to Moses, "I am who I am." He said further, "Thus you shall say to the Israelites, 'I am has sent me to you.' " . . .

Then Moses answered, "But suppose they do not believe me or listen to me, but say, 'The LORD did not appear to you.' " The Lord said to him, "What is that in your hand?" He said, "A staff." And he said, "Throw it on the ground." So he threw the staff on the ground, and it became a snake; and Moses drew back from it. Then the LORD said to Moses, "Reach out your hand, and seize it by the tail"—so he reached out his hand and grasped it, and it became a staff in his hand—"so that they may believe that the LORD, the God of their ancestors, the God of Abraham, the God of Isaac, and the God of Jacob, has appeared to you." . . .

But Moses said to the LORD, "O my Lord, I have never been eloquent, neither in the past nor even now that you have spoken to your servant; but I am slow of speech and slow of tongue." Then the LORD said to him, "Who gives speech to mortals? Who makes them mute or deaf, seeing or blind? Is it not I, the LORD? Now go, and I will be with your mouth and teach you what you are to speak." But he said, "O my Lord, please send someone else."

—Ex. 3:9–14; 4:1–5, 10–13

For the past three years, on the Monday before Thanksgiving, Arlene Sands has closed the Sandbox Café at two in the afternoon. This is so that the Sandbox can be a gathering place for what has become a very special Thanksgiving celebration. Arlene then spends the afternoon cleaning and arranging the place. The floors must be spotless, the smoky haze must be removed from the windows. The tables must be waxed and then covered with tablecloths. And, of course, the food must be prepared.

This year, Arlene began her ritual again by stuffing two large turkeys with sage dressing, much like her mother used to make. She remembered how her mother would get up early in the morning and pull this huge bird out of the refrigerator. She made a special stuffing with bread, onions, cranberries and sage, all cooked in butter and a variety of other seasonings. The smell of the stuffing would permeate the house early on Thanksgiving Day, luring Arlene and her two brothers out of their beds and into the kitchen.

What always struck Arlene was how much time her mom put into this special meal. It was a huge undertaking that began at five or six in the morning and continued until guests began arriving late in the afternoon. But it wasn't over even then, for there was the serving of the meal and then several hours of cleaning up. All told, Arlene's mom would often spend fifteen hours preparing, serving, and cleaning up this meal.

At least twenty people always came—family who lived close by and a few neighbors and some business acquaintances. All of them came to feast on a huge variety of home-cooked foods, which filled the table to overflowing. Even though her family was not wealthy and many times had to struggle just to put a regular meal on the table, the Thanksgiving feast was always a wonder to behold.

When Arlene was in high school, she finally asked her mom why she did this every year. "Well," her mom replied, stirring the gravy as it bubbled in the pan, "the Lord has certainly kept us fed through the year. Kept us warm. Kept us together. The very least I can do is to say thanks by making a meal for a few friends and family. I always hope the meal says two things. Number one is, thanks to God for caring for us. And number two is, I love my family and my friends."

Arlene remembered that conversation. And when she moved to Gateway she decided that she needed to continue that wonderful tradition. There were a handful of students and a few neighbors who really helped her get started, so the meal began as a thank you to them. From there it expanded, and now, three years later, anyone who wanted to bring a dish to share was welcome. Somehow, everyone always fit in the restaurant—last year about forty folks. Arlene always cooked the turkeys just to say thanks—to God for blessing her another year, and to her friends for supporting her.

By five o'clock Arlene had finished her cleaning and arranging. She took one more look around the room to make sure that everything was in place. The silverware sparkled on the white linen tablecloths. The glasses reflected the lights overhead as well as the candles set on each table amid an arrangement of leaves, nuts, and dried flowers. Off to the side was the long serving table covered in white with serving spoons and hot mats scattered on it. At each end there was a large fork and knife where the turkeys would be carved. Arlene turned down the lights and took in a deep breath. The smell of the turkeys carried with it the joy-filled memories of her first Thanksgiving in Gateway.

About six o'clock, the guests began arriving. Melanie and Claris got there first. Melanie brought glazed carrots. This was not an old traditional recipe but one she had found in a cookbook a few years back. Some time ago she had wanted to bring something really different to a potluck dinner her friends were having. She knew they would be bringing chicken, pizza, or baked beans. She scoured through the cookbooks in the library until she came upon a recipe for glazed carrots with honey and mustard. They were the hit of the party. No one could believe that Melanie had actually baked them herself. For her, it became a symbol of her independence. She could make her own decisions, take care of herself. She baked glazed carrots.

Claris brought wild rice. This was a traditional dish, handed down for several generations, from when her family lived in the Deep South and raised rice. Her great-grandfather planted a special patch of rice, just a small section, which was grown for the family to use over the holidays. It was expensive to buy the seed, but he always felt it was worth it. So wild rice became the tradition for Claris's family to remind them of their roots and the hard times that they had been through.

Dr. Evans brought a potato casserole. He loved potatoes and was always looking for something interesting to do with them. Long ago he had tired of the same, plain mashed potatoes so he began making them with cheese and onions and mayonnaise. Then he found he could add all sorts of interesting things like vegetables, or meat, or soup. He baked, broiled, fried, and boiled. He sliced, diced, and mashed. And each year for this Thanksgiving banquet he tried out a new recipe. This one had three different kinds of cheese mixed with peas and carrots.

Brad brought cranberry relish. His mother made this dish every Thanksgiving—that is, every year except 1986. She just didn't have time to make the relish that year, having just given birth to twins, and with the flood the week before. So she bought a can of jelled cranberry sauce and plunked it into the cut glass dish. Brad was horrified when he saw it sitting on the table with little indentations running around its middle. What was Thanksgiving coming to? You don't "buy" cranberry sauce! Everything has to be made . . . right in the kitchen! This was not right! He looked forward to a turkey baked in their oven. Mashed potatoes, sweet potatoes, beans, rolls and pumpkin pie made in their kitchen. These are the things that make Thanksgiving . . . *Thanksgiving*!

Brad could barely get through that meal back in 1986. He wondered what else might be changed. He looked suspiciously at the stuffing, picking through it, sniffing it, finally putting a small bit of it into his mouth. Satisfied that this was, indeed, homemade, he did the same with everything else that was served. His mother, noticing his suspicious manner, tried to assure him that everything else was homemade, but his trust had been shattered. When he went away to college, he needed this reminder that nothing had really changed, which is why he brought homemade cranberry relish.

Annie came in a little out of breath. The bread she made took longer to bake than she had expected, so as soon as it was done, she hurriedly wrapped the loaves in towels and rushed over to the Sandbox. The AIDS virus was wearing her down, but she kept on pushing. She thought this might be her last Thanksgiving and she wanted to do something special, but she didn't know exactly what. She finally decided that bread would be very symbolic—the staff of life, nourishment for body and soul, and, of course, the Last Supper. She wanted somehow to be sure she could take with her all the friendships gathered around these tables. She wanted all her friends also to take a part of her with them. So she mixed the dough by hand, kneading it slowly, filling it with as much love as she could. And when the dough was satiny smooth, she carefully shaped it into three big, soft ovals and placed them on the cornmeal-covered tray. Now her friends watched her as she carefully unwrapped the loaves and placed them on the table.

Martha Gibbons brought the desserts. She spent almost three days baking these wonderful, rich creations—pies, cakes, and a soon-to-be-flaming plum pudding. The desserts would be topped with whipped cream or hard sauce, or drizzled with warm chocolate syrup. Martha had always felt that desserts were her real forte. The other parts of the meal were meant for nutrition, but the dessert was something extra, a way of indulging oneself. Desserts were meant to caress the palate, which in turn gave a sort of "back rub" to the soul.

Forty-two people brought some Thanksgiving memory to share with all the others. When the overhead lights were turned off and the room was lit only by the glow of several dozen candles, a peculiar warmth was generated. As the guests stood in silence amid the flickering shadows, a feeling of closeness grew, connecting each one to the other. Arlene prayed, thanking God for the blessings of another year and the gifts of good friends. And then the room was filled with laughter and stories and songs celebrating life together.

■ ■ ■

In his book *The Fifth Discipline,* Peter Senge describes what he calls "systems thinking." Everything is connected together in an organization, and organizations are linked together as well. Consider the insides of an old clock with all its gears. A church may be one gear. If that gear is not functioning properly, our tendency is to look at the gear itself and then the gears on either side of it. We check to make sure there is no dust, that all the cogs are there, that there is sufficient lubrication. We clean them, maybe even replace them. If all that doesn't fix the problem we either give up or try it all over again. Systems thinking suggests that the problem may not be with our organization or with the organizations right next to us. It may be all the way at the other end of the system. Checking back with each preceding gear, we finally find one that has a cog missing. Replacing that one gear makes all the rest run better.

> Systems thinking also shows that small, well-focused actions can sometimes produce significant, enduring improvements, if they're in the right place. Systems thinkers refer to this principle as "leverage."
>
> Tackling a difficult problem is often a matter of seeing where the high leverage lies, a change which—with minimum of effort—would lead to lasting, significant improvement.[1]

In chapter 2 we looked at some of the problems that face the church today. In this chapter I want to address those problems and paint a picture of what the church might look like in the future. I do this because the problems in campus ministries are related to and sometimes caused

1. Peter M. Senge, *The Fifth Discipline: The Art and Practice of the Learning Organization* (New York: Currency/Doubleday, 1990), p. 634.

by problems in the churches. Many young men and women come to campus with a negative attitude toward organized religion already instilled in them from their experiences with worship and Sunday schools over the past eighteen years. To be more effective in helping *college students* in their shipwreck of faith, we must be more effective in helping our *children* understand their faith.

In the interviews, quite a few students said they thought the church was boring and irrelevant. Most of them were either forced or expected to go to church and Sunday school. A great many of them considered both to be a waste of time. Pastors, teachers, and parents were unable to make faith real to this generation. Instead, they were sometimes frightened by images of hell and screaming dead bodies, or they were chided for asking too many questions, or they were generally ignored in worship except for those special occasions when the children's choir sang or the minister did a children's sermon.

▪ ▪ ▪

I can think of what the perfect worship service would be for me and I would feel so wonderful. We would need a lot of singing and just a lot of praise, a lot of joy. And I feel like church is just so boring. It is so drab. And, I mean, spirituality is such an amazing, wonderful thing, it's so exciting. And yet when you go to church and worship it seems completely the opposite. I would want it to feel like a definite communion between the pastor and the people and the Earth and our surroundings and the music. I think everything is so connected, and it frustrates me when I go to church and we sit this far apart on the pews, fold our hands, and just kind of look at our bulletins. And it just seems so completely contradictory to what God is in my opinion. (18-year-old female, freshman, Presbyterian)

▪ ▪ ▪

Now, I don't want to give the impression that every student had such negative experiences. There are churches where children enjoy going to Sunday school and worship. It is to these stories that I want to turn to look for some clues about how to make the church exciting and relevant not only to our children, but to our adults—young and old—as well.

College students want faith to be connected to the real world. If what we do on Sunday, or Friday, or Saturday has no connection with school, work, sports, recreation, music, eating, or family, then what is the point? And I would have to agree. Ever since Constantine ended the persecution of Christians in the fourth century, we have gotten lazier and lazier in recognizing our faith as the foundation for everything we do. In a conversation with a professor at JMU who was telling me how meaningful her faith was, I asked her what role her faith played in her teaching. She said it played no role.

In order to reconnect our religious faith with our secular lives we will need to make some changes in both the reasons we do things in church and the way we do things in church. I want to spend the rest of this chapter looking at various components of the church experience in relation to problems of healthy, normal transitions of faith and making religious beliefs relevant and exciting.

Worship

One of the biggest fears people have of change is losing those traditions that have meant so much to them. There is usually considerable anger when someone suggests replacing all of the music in a service with contemporary music—rock, folk, country, jazz, or even gospel. The interviews have suggested that most students aren't so interested in trashing *all* the traditions. They do, however, want to know *why* this or that tradition is important. "Why do we do this?"

▪ ▪ ▪

I remember when I was ten, eleven, twelve years old. I remember really not enjoying it (worship). I remember being bored, just sitting there. And my mom would tell me, "Well, if you pay attention to what the pastor is saying it's going to be interesting." And I would pay attention to what the pastor was saying and he would get up there and it would be like the Charlie Brown thing (garbled clarinet sound). And I was just like, "What are you talking about?" It didn't affect me in any way. It didn't reach me in any way. (20-year-old male, sophomore, Roman Catholic)

▪ ▪ ▪

My little sister's been going to Sunday school. But they don't know the Lord's Prayer and the Gloria Patri and stuff like that. And I thought it was so funny, because I never realized what the words meant when I learned them—I think I've known them my entire life—and I'm like, that's really strange. It's just like we're being almost brainwashed. We just . . . repeat things. We don't even realize what we're saying. So I was kind of proud of them in a way for not learning them. It gives them more time to think about what they're saying. (19-year-old female, sophomore, Christian)

▪ ▪ ▪

We do a great disservice to our children when we plod through a service without ever stopping to remind each other of the meanings in all the pieces. We have become so intent on getting through the order of worship that we forget that many people in the congregation, not just youth and young adults, don't know why we do what we do. To review, at each service, a little bit of the human story behind a hymn, a prayer, a creed, is to bring that great big impersonal church story into individual lives.

There are some traditions that have lost their meaning. The times have changed, the culture has changed. I am reminded of the story of the woman whose daughter came into the kitchen while she was pulling the roast out of the oven. The daughter noticed that there were two pans, one with a large roast in it, the other with a small end that had been cut off. The daughter asked her mother why she always cut the end off the roast. Her mother said, "Well, that's the way my mother always cooked it, and it always turned out quite delicious. So I have followed the exact same recipe." The daughter was curious and went from the kitchen to the living room where her grandmother was sitting, waiting for dinner. The daughter asked her grandmother, "Grandma, why did you always cut the end of the roast off and cook it separately?" The grandmother thought about this for a minute and then suddenly remembered why. "Because I only had a small pan, and that was the only way the roast would fit!"

There are traditions in our churches that are much like cutting off the end of the roast beef. At one time they had real meaning and purpose. But with the changing times, that meaning and purpose has been lost. Such traditions may be things like the time of the service, or the day of the week, the order of the service, the songs we sing, or the leadership of the service. The question to be asked on a regular basis is, "If we weren't doing it this way now, would we start?" This gives a fresh perspective to everything we do. It forces us to imagine *not* doing something and then asks us to justify doing it.

Our reasons for worship need to be reexamined as well. As I said in the second chapter, God does not need our worship to exist. And God does not demand our worship in order for us to "earn" our salvation. Worship is supposed to revitalize us so that we can live our faith in the world. Bruce Reed, in his book *The Task of the Church and the Role of Its Members*, develops the oscillation theory from research done by the Grubb Institute in London, England.[2] Reed says that we move back-and-forth between intra-dependence and extra-dependence. He defines intra-dependence as a state of being dependent on oneself, drawing from

2. Bruce Reed, *The Task of the Church and the Role of Its Members* (London: The Grubb Institute, June 1975), p. 3.

one's inner resources. Extra-dependence is the state of being dependent on someone outside of oneself. He uses the example of a child and his mother going to the park. For a time, the child sits on his mother's lap until he feels comfortable enough to venture a short distance away. He plays for a while, then hurts himself and comes running back to Mom. After she holds him, kisses him, reassures him, he is, once again, ready to go out and play. This back-and-forth pattern between extra-dependence and intra-dependence continues for the afternoon.

Our worship experience operates in a similar way. We spend the week out in the world with our energies being slowly used up—we are intra-dependent. We are wounded in our dealings with people. We lose sight of why we are doing what we do. We come to worship to be reenergized, healed, reminded of the vision and sent back out—we are extra-dependent. It is like being shot out of a cannon into the week. We start out with our energies high, the vision alive and vibrant, but by midweek we begin to lose that momentum. By Friday and Saturday we are desperate for renewal.

That renewal comes in the form of a caring community who will bind up our wounds, listen to our complaints, restore our confidence. It is the unconditional acceptance, the open arms, the warm smile. It is gratitude for work well done and excitement for the work that lies ahead. The Thanksgiving dinner provided by Arlene Sands created that sort of renewal in her guests.

That renewal comes in the form of a pastor and a choir who sing songs and tell stories that remind us of the vision. It is the vision found in our Scriptures from Genesis through Revelation. It is the Garden of Eden, the New Jerusalem. This is what we try so hard every week to make our world look like. This is how God intended humans to live in the creation.

That renewal comes in the form of hymns and songs and prayers and creeds that fill us with the excitement of the faith. It is the connections with people of faith down through the centuries. It is the thunder and lightening from the great cloud of witnesses spread not only through time but around the Earth.

And then we are sent back out to our various ministries. And as I said in the last chapter, each one of us is called to a ministry. We are called to be mothers and fathers, sisters and brothers, sons and daughters. We are called to be teachers and doctors and lawyers and salesclerks. We are called to be friends and colleagues. We are called to be students. And this worship service must somehow say what faith looks like in those ministries. What does it mean to be a parent and a person of faith? What does it mean to be a carpenter and a person of faith? What does it mean to be a student in elementary school and a person of faith? This is faith connected to the real world.

Tim Harrison, associate pastor with youth and their families at Whitworth Community Presbyterian Church in Spokane, Washington, writes about how he has involved youth in his worship services and the results of that involvement:

> Our church has doubled in worship attendance in 5 years, from 650 to 1300 each Sunday (membership about 980). On any given Sunday, we have 200+ youth in church, many of whom are not members. We (the session/pastors) have some ideas on why God is causing growth.
>
> 1. Our preaching is biblically-based, with real applications and challenges. We use several (3–5) illustrations. We speak to youth, because many adults seeking a return to the faith do not understand church-eze language either. (Earl Palmer, a gifted preacher in our denomination, says we should target our preaching to high school students).
> 2. Contemporary worship services (we now have 2) with music that is not cheesy camp songs or too complicated to sing. The services are lay-led, with a strong emphasis on developing leadership. (This is where most of our youth get involved.) The services are a great reflection of our Reformed heritage through use of Scripture as prayer, affirmation, assurance of pardon, calls to worship, etc. Whenever we added a service, it filled up within a year. We are adding a fifth service next fall. (Yes, we are very tired!)
> 3. Real lay leadership. Youth-led worship, really! They share the prayers, read the text, play the instruments, lead the singing, share in mission minutes, usher, teach Sunday School, serve on committees. They do this alongside adults as equals, not as "sub-leaders."[3]

We make a lot of excuses for not adding excitement to the worship services. We make a lot of excuses for not allowing children and youth to have meaningful roles in the planning and leading of worship. One that we Presbyterians like to cite is Paul's admonition that "all things should

---

3. Tim Harrison, Associate Pastor with Youth and Their Families, Whitworth Community Presbyterian Church, Spokane, WA. From a note in the Presbyterian Youth Connection (PYC) meeting on Presbynet. Used by permission.

be done decently and in order" (1 Cor. 14:40). Reading Paul's description, one gets a feeling that worship services at that time were complete chaos with lots of people speaking at once, some of them in tongues, some interpreting, some prophesying. A little more enthusiastic disorder in most worship services today would not be harmful.

Confirmation

In middle school when it was time to go through Confirmation and I couldn't go to Sunday school anymore, I had to sit through the sermon and everything in church . . . and I hated that! I was like, "This is really stupid. I don't want to do this. This is pointless and has no bearing on my life." My parents made me go to Confirmation. They decided that they wanted both me and my brother to be confirmed and after that we could choose whether or not . . . to believe in it. I think that was a really good decision on my mother's part because if I hadn't done that, I would've given up a long time ago. (18-year-old female, freshman, Presbyterian)

■ ■ ■

Most of the Christian students interviewed were confirmed or baptized in their early teens. (Some denominations use confirmation as the ritual for full membership, others use baptism.) This seems to be about the time they might be making a transition from Fowler's stage 2 (Mythic–Literal) to stage 3 (Synthetic–Conventional). What many church leaders have also noticed is that, following these rituals of membership, a large percentage of those students become inactive, some never entering the church again. This, it seems to me, is a clear indication that something is not right with the whole process of confirmation. Tim Harrison, again, writes about his church's changes in the confirmation process:

> We broke the trend the past two years. We have a 100% retention rate from the last 2 classes! (one moved away, but is active in another church). 100% of those youth are at least in worship regularly, and most serve our church on committees, leading Sunday School or Jr. High/Grade School youth programs, or are peer leaders in the high school programs. Here is what we changed:
>
> 1. High school only. Developmental issues, understanding commitment, relational issues (covenanting with a group), communication skills.

2. Emphasis on the class as an individual process, not a right of passage. Parent's meeting at the beginning highlights that this is the teenager's choice, and parents can encourage but not force.
3. Take commitment seriously. For instance, this year a guy (junior in high school) dropped out the last week because he said he was not ready to take his faith seriously. I told him I had the utmost respect for him because he was showing real integrity. He knows my care for him is not dependent on his performance in the class. Each year we've had people drop, and some have joined another year, but some have not. Youth must be able to reject faith if they are truly able to embrace it.
4. Teach faith as a process that actually requires your brain. We look at Genesis 1 and 2, two different Creation accounts, and then talk about how we are able to make sense of understanding God as Creator. The faith process includes disciplines like prayer, studying the Bible, seeking justice, etc.
5. Group covenant. I, as the pastor, am not the gatekeeper for the church. They are the church, and I am coming alongside them as they understand how they might live and work as the body.
6. Ask lots of questions!!!!! If you are not interested in worshiping God, why do you want to join the body of Christ? Can you share the gospel without seeking justice? How? Why and how are you going to be involved in the body of Christ next year?[4]

Confirmation, baptism, bar or bat mitzvah and other initiation rites need to be seen as the beginnings of adult life in the religious community. These rites do not automatically give a person a mature adult faith, which both the individual and the congregation need to understand. Instead they represent the opening of the door to a journey that will *lead them to* that maturity of faith. The responsibility is not that of the youth alone. It is a responsibility shared by all the members of that religious community. What Tim Harrison did in his church was recognize the developmental needs of his youth and then create a program that fit those needs. This was not just filling their heads with information. Rather it helped them understand the whys as well as the whats. It allowed them to take responsibility for their faith life by asking questions and making their own decisions.

4. Ibid.

Leadership

> The gifts [Christ] gave were that some would be apostles, some prophets, some evangelists, some pastors and teachers, to equip the saints for the work of ministry, for building up the body of Christ. (Eph. 4:11–12)

Ninety percent of the leaders [of Youth Explosion] went to college, so we figured, that's a good thing! None of us were thinking about college when we first started. It boosted our grades. My grades went like crazy when I started doing this. All the time we were telling these little kids, "You have to do your homework, and you can't come and sing in the choir unless you do this." So, we were telling them one thing and we couldn't go and be knuckleheads in school.

We weren't even thinking that our whole lives were changing while we were doing this. But then we were about to graduate we all kind of sat down and said, "Look at all this stuff we're doing!" We were getting scholarships and money from all over the place, the city was recognizing us individually, and then we all went to college and had no clue how we got there! But I really think it was because of Youth Explosion and because we had to be role models for little kids. (21-year-old female, senior, Baptist)

▪ ▪ ▪

Congregations need to encourage their children and youth to take meaningful leadership roles. In the Presbyterian Church (U.S.A.), when Youth join the church "they are commissioned for *full participation* in the mission and the *governance* of the church . . . . " (italics added)[5] This is true in many religious organizations. But we cannot expect that they will suddenly be given all of the wonderful gifts of leadership when they become members. Even Moses had to have some guidance as he learned how to best lead the Israelites (Exodus 18). Children and youth need to have adults who will help them develop the practical skills they will use to connect their faith with the ministries to which they have been called.

The advantages to developing children and youth as leaders in the church go far beyond adding excitement to the worship service. Though the story about the young woman involved with Youth Explosion is an unusual one, it nevertheless illustrates the power the church has to transform lives in a very real way. Self-esteem was raised, along with

---

5. *Book of Order.* The Constitution of the Presbyterian Church (U.S.A.) (Louisville, KY: Office of the General Assembly, Presbyterian Church (U.S.A.), 1997–98), W-4.2003.

school grades. Young men and women who never thought college was an option suddenly found themselves to be recipients of scholarships. When we trust that God's Spirit is alive and working in our children and youth, then we allow them not only to see but experience faith's connection with everyday life.

Sunday School

> You shall put these words of mine in your heart and soul, and you shall bind them as a sign on your hand, and fix them as an emblem on your forehead. Teach them to your children, talking about them when you are at home and when you are away, when you lie down and when you rise. (Deut. 11:18, 19)

We need to do a better job of inviting questions. And when those questions come we must resist the temptation to provide instant, pat answers. We must turn back the myth that our students will lose all respect for us if we sometimes answer their tough questions with "I don't know."

We must allow our people time to think, to wrestle with the issues, as Jesus often did.

And we can create a better thinking climate by encouraging students to ask one another questions, by letting them forget we're the teachers for a while. Let them be the askers.

> Educator and author Jane Healy said, "The teacher has to be able to stop dispensing information long enough to listen to the children, listen and encourage the children's questions."[6]

One of the most important factors in students deciding to stay or not to stay in the church is whether they had a meaningful relationship with an adult, many of whom were Sunday school teachers. In almost every student who had remained active there was a Sunday school teacher, youth leader, or pastor who had made a personal connection with them. We spend a great deal of time developing new curriculum that has little impact on the child. Of far more value would be encouraging teachers, maybe even *teaching* teachers, how to develop healthy, helpful relationships with their students. Most often, Sunday school teachers are not professionally trained. They have graciously volunteered to help out in an

6. Thom and Joani Schultz, *Why Nobody Learns Much of Anything at Church: And How to Fix It* (Loveland, CO: Group, 1994), p. 96.

endeavor that they consider to be very important. The church gives them a curriculum with a student book and a teacher's guide and says, "Here is the plan for the spring or the fall." The teacher may receive some training about how to do the crafts, or some background about the Bible, or some instruction on how to move through the various components of the lesson. But even with all that training and preparation, most of the students I interviewed found Sunday school to be a very negative experience and often cited it as one of the reasons, if not *the* reason, for their leaving the church.

> Sitting down in front of a heaping plate of fatty, high-cholesterol food was a happy habit for millions. "Why change? I like this food!" they cried. They were oblivious to the fact that they were gradually clogging their arteries and slicing years off their lives. They were suffering from a disease they didn't know they had, treading down a dangerous alley with no cognizance of what lurked in the darkness.
>
> Similarly the church is slowly suffocating itself even though it's largely oblivious to unhealthy habits.
>
> We must sound the alarm. We must jolt the church into recognizing its self-destructive habits of education. The church doesn't realize it's infected with a life-draining disease.[7]

Here, again, most churches have no idea or the wrong idea of what Sunday school is supposed to be doing. Sunday school should be another place where people learn about the connections between faith and real life. To teach children, we must have an understanding of where they are in their faith development. A child's faith does not look like an adult faith. A child's understanding and assessment of the world around him or her is going to be different from that of an adult. Our teaching must reflect those differences if we are truly interested in engaging children in the journey of faith.

Our churches, synagogues, and temples were once the center of our communities. It is time for us to reclaim that position. Not because the pastor, rabbi, or priest is the only educated person or has the "keys" to salvation, but because here is where the vision of community originates. Here is where we are strengthened to go out into the world. Here is where we are healed and reenergized when we come back from the world.

---

7. Ibid., p. 210.

Questions for Reflection

1. As a child, what were your experiences of worship? How did the pastor or congregation involve you or communicate with you?
2. What do you remember about confirmation or baptism? Was it a meaningful experience? Why or why not?
3. What leadership roles did you or other children and youth play in your church? Who were the adults who helped you and how did they help?
4. Who were some significant adult leaders in your church? What made them effective leaders?
5. What was your experience of Sunday school? Why was it that way?
6. Were there any Sunday school teachers you thought were particularly effective? What did they do that was helpful?
7. What does a faith that is connected to the real world look like?

8

Equipped for Every Good Work

Now you have observed my teaching, my conduct, my aim in life, my faith, my patience, my love, my steadfastness, my persecutions and suffering the things that happened to me in Antioch, Iconium, and Lystra. What persecutions I endured! Yet the Lord rescued me from all of them. Indeed, all who want to live a godly life in Christ Jesus will be persecuted. But wicked people and impostors will go from bad to worse, deceiving others and being deceived. But as for you, continue in what you have learned and firmly believed, knowing from whom you learned it, and how from childhood you have known the sacred writings that are able to instruct you for salvation through faith in Christ Jesus. All scripture is inspired by God and is useful for teaching, for reproof, for correction, and for training in righteousness, so that everyone who belongs to God may be proficient, equipped for every good work.

—2 Tim. 3:10–17

It was Saturday night and Born Under a Rock was playing at Nitty Gritty's, the local hangout in Gateway. The place was packed with people celebrating Monthaven's first football victory in seven years. It seemed as though everyone on campus was there listening to the chainsawlike music that Born Under a Rock cranked out at ear-splitting levels. No one could understand the words. They didn't care. But when the band got to the chorus of "One Step from the Bottom," well, the song took on anthem status with everyone joining in, singing at the top of their lungs: "We use ta be one step from the bottom, yeah, one step from the bottom, na, na, na, one step from the bottom . . . " The rest of the words were gibberish because people still couldn't figure them out. There was some suspicion that Leather, the lead singer, didn't know them either.

James had arrived at Nitty Gritty's early in the evening. He had wanted to be alone, and wherever Born Under a Rock was playing was usually a good place to find solitude. But at ten o'clock the doors suddenly burst open and a swarm of people packed themselves in shoulder to chin, with everyone slapping each other on the back and trying to give "high-fives" without spilling their beer. James kept hoping that the commotion would pass quickly, but it just kept going. Being a somewhat shy person, he tucked himself deep into a corner of the bar rather than try to fight the crowd. He figured no one would notice him there in the shadows.

It was almost three-thirty in the morning when James finally felt comfortable enough to wind his way through the handful of people who remained as Leather tried to remember the words to "One Step from the Bottom." James stepped outside into the cool October air, his ears ringing from the musical massacre he had endured for more than six hours. He took a long, deep breath and then, rather than heading for the residence hall, he turned left and walked toward the edge of town.

The storefronts of downtown Gateway gradually turned to beautifully manicured lawns dusted with the crisp, golden leaves of stately maples. James turned and walked through the old neighborhood, not really noticing the thick white columns standing like sentinels in front of many of the houses. The early morning had swallowed up the din of the night before and he wandered aimlessly in the refreshing silence.

As the first rays of the sun turned the sugar maples a brilliant yellow, James found a park bench and sat down. He hadn't been there long when a cheery voice said, "Good morning!" and Lily Greenston sat down beside him.

Lily had lived in Gateway most of her ninety-seven years. After her husband died in 1972, she had begun taking early morning walks partly for the exercise and partly to keep her mind off the memories of her beloved spouse. On one of those mornings, she had walked through the Monthaven campus and ended up having a delightful conversation with two students who were stretching before their morning run. As the years passed, she became a sort of grandmother to many of the students. She would catch up with them on her morning walks, or they would stop by her home for milk and home-made cookies. Lily would talk with them about the early days of Monthaven and they would tell her about the new class schedules, or difficulties with parents or boyfriends or girlfriends.

Lily had a way of knowing when the conversation could be about the weather or when a person really needed to talk. That was one of the things the students really appreciated about her. She would just appear at the most opportune times ready to sit down and listen to whatever might be on someone's mind. And, of course, any student sitting on a park bench at seven o'clock on a Sunday morning had serious thoughts he was pondering. So Lily sat down next to James.

A long silence followed her initial greeting. Finally,she asked, "What are you thinking about?"

It was as though someone had pulled the plug on the Hoover Dam. James burst forth with a tidal wave of his deepest thoughts. They poured out in no particular sequence, random thoughts gushing out into the gentle morning. He was a junior. He didn't know what he wanted to do. His father wanted him to go to dental school. His mother thought he would be a great teacher. His minister said he had a great way with people and should consider a career in counseling. His father wanted him to go into dental practice with him. He didn't like biology. He liked children, but was mostly afraid of them. He didn't know if God existed. He liked antique cars and wanted to work on them like his grandfather did. He wasn't sure why he was even in school.

Lily listened carefully, trying to rearrange all the bits of information into some sort of order. When, at last, it seemed the flood was over, there was silence. James thought to himself, Oh, God, what have I done? I don't even know this old woman. She probably thinks I'm a nut case.

Lily thought carefully and then stretched her hand toward James.

"We haven't even introduced ourselves. I'm Lily Greenston."

James weakly shook her hand.

"Nice to meet you, Ms. Greenston. I'm James Holloway."

"Well, it is nice to meet you, James. And please call me Lily. All the other students do."

James felt better. There was something in Lily's voice and manner that helped him relax. He looked at her face, framed in whispy gray hair, etched with deep lines, punctuated by thin lips that were accustomed to smiling and eyes that still sparkled.

"I just wish I knew what I was supposed to be doing."

Lily took his hand again. "James, when I was your age I was married, had two children and a third on the way. We lived in a farmhouse just north of here and worked from sunup 'til sundown every day of the year just to barely survive. I can remember many times bent over out in the fields asking the same question. 'What am I supposed to be doing?' There were any number of nights when I sat in the rocking chair with a child in my arms wondering if this was all there was.

"Well, what did you do?"

"I did lots of things. While the children were growing up, I worked on the farm. Once they were all in school, I took a job in town working as an administrative secretary for the railroad. A few years later, I opened up a little fabric shop. That didn't do so well, so I went and worked for McFarlane Seed Company. I worked there until I retired in 1967. I still didn't think I was doing what I was supposed to be doing. It just never seemed like the right fit.

"My husband died in 1972. I've got seven children, one was killed in World War II and one died of cancer. I have thirty-six grandchildren and fourteen great-grandchildren and I finally feel as though I'm doing what I'm supposed to be doing."

"What are you doing?" asked James.

"Talking with you."

▪ ▪ ▪

Lily is one of those people who has a passion for college students. Without any formal program, she is willing to sit down and connect with students. She is a mentor to some, a friend to many. The most important aspect of any program created by a congregation or a campus ministry is that willingness to develop personal relationships. Though it may never appear on paper, it should be the primary focus of pastors, congregation members, and students.

In this section I would like to outline some specific programs in which we are currently engaged at James Madison University or that are being executed on other campuses with some degree of success. No program can or should simply be taken from one group and "installed" into another without considering all its many ingredients and processes. I present these programs as suggestions that, with some twisting and turning, may also work on other campuses and in other situations. I would hope that the creative process would be applied before making any adaptations.

Worship

"For this reason they are before the throne of God,
  and worship him day and night within his temple,
  and the one who is seated on the throne will shelter them.
They will hunger no more, and thirst no more;
  the sun will not strike them,
  nor any scorching heat;
for the Lamb at the center of the throne will be their shepherd,
  and he will guide them to the springs of the water of life,
and God will wipe away every tear from their eyes."

—Rev. 7:15–17

When I was doing an internship at Pace Memorial United Methodist Church in Richmond, the pastor there, Dr. Richard Soulen, said that worship should be the center of the church because out of worship comes everything else. That made a lot of sense to me back then and has become the underlying foundation for what we do in worship. The worship experience should be one that inspires people to go out and do their ministry.

Our worship team at JMU meets once a week to plan the Sunday celebrations that are held Sunday evenings. Some semesters we have a set format for the service, other semesters we don't. We are very experimental and very experiential, drawing on all sorts of resources to explore what faith looks like on a college campus. We have used play dough, paint, cotton balls, colored paper, and an assortment of other craft materials to help students talk about what they believe and why. We use a variety of music from traditional hymns to contemporary folk, country, and pop. I do not preach a sermon; I tell a story. You have been reading parts of some of the stories as introductions to each chapter of this book. The stories are based on real people or combinations of folks, but I always try to illustrate what faith looks like in ordinary folks in their everyday lives.

We try to create a welcoming atmosphere not only emotionally but physically. The lighting needs to be warm. Since bright fluorescent lights are too cold, we use incandescent whenever possible. We try to always have something baking in the oven. Communion bread creates an especially welcoming smell. We usually have some sort of music playing in the background that will set the tone for the service. Recently, our folks have gotten interested in Irish folk music. And, most important, our leaders try to speak with every person who attends.

We have tried to address the complaints most students have about worship. Do we have hundreds of students attending these bold departures from the norm? No. We get a dozen or so, maybe twenty. We have found that those who come to worship like having this small, close-knit group. It is the way they find worship meaningful, so we will not change it.

Mentors

> When they had crossed, Elijah said to Elisha, "Tell me what I may do for you, before I am taken from you." Elisha said, "Please let me inherit a double share of your spirit." He responded, "You have asked a hard thing; yet, if you see me as I am being taken from you, it will be granted you; if not, it will not." As they continued walking and talking, a chariot of fire and horses of fire separated the two of them, and Elijah ascended in a whirlwind into heaven. Elisha kept watching and crying out, "Father, father! The chariots of Israel and its horsemen!" But when he could no longer see him, he grasped his own clothes and tore them in two pieces.
>
> He picked up the mantle of Elijah that had fallen from him, and went back and stood on the bank of the Jordan. He took the mantle of Elijah that had fallen from him, and struck the water, saying, "Where is the Lord, the God of Elijah?" When he had struck the water, the water was parted to the one side and to the other, and Elisha went over. (2 Kings 2:9–14)

> One characteristic I esteem highly in defining a mentor is someone who accompanies an individual on their journey of leadership development. This accompanying process includes monitoring, teaching, modeling and pacing the journey. The mentor is someone who positively influences and someone who is esteemed by the one who needs to be mentored.[1]

The most important program we can develop for college students is mentoring. As children, we watch adults very carefully. We scrutinize every action, every word. We mimic what adults do, what they say, how they respond to the world. This same careful observation continues into

1. Dr. Ira V. Frazier, "A Faith-Based Mentoring Program" (www.indiana.edu/~rugsdev/faith.html).

our teen years and we begin to select specific adults whom we will emulate very carefully. Sunday after Sunday, I can remember watching one of our youth advisers, Don McKinney. I thought he was the greatest person. He was thoughtful and thought-provoking. He was gentle and good-humored. He was laid back in his discussions with us teenagers. It wasn't until after I had graduated from seminary that I realized what a powerful influence he'd been. I attribute my desire to work with youth and young adults to him. I also find myself thinking about how he might respond in various situations. He was sort of a mentor to me, and continues to be without his even knowing it!

I say that Don was "sort of" a mentor to me because a real mentor relationship needs to be two ways. There must be communication back and forth. There must be a recognized relationship, although the two participants don't have to call it a "mentor" relationship.

The most effective mentor relationships are informal. Various studies have shown that assigned mentors don't work as well because there is no common bond. Mentor relationships develop as two people participate in some common activity. I continue to be a mentor to a student who was involved with me in Habitat for Humanity. I am a mentor with another student who is in our music program. We come together to do some task, but we have opportunities for conversations along the way. Questions arise about meaning and direction from within the context of what we are doing.

But the one being mentored cannot be the only one benefiting from such a relationship. The mentor must also find some benefit. Elisha was mentored by Elijah. The benefit to Elijah was that he would have someone to pass his prophetic mantel to when he was finished. I am sure that there was also a sense of companionship, a person with whom Elijah could share his joys and frustrations. Mentor and mentee have a degree of equalness between them, valuing each other's ideas and opinions, affirming the other's innermost being.

> The faith community is a logical place as a store house for mentoring relationships. Considering the various auxiliaries and the numerous pools of volunteers, there is dynamic need for mentoring relationships. The volunteers are mainly adult learners who need training and instruction. The training and support for adults at different stages of life, along with the development of the community's mission, can find mentoring to be an ideal training method.[2]

2. Ibid.

Here is a wonderful way for churches to make contact with college students and support campus ministries. But this means that church members will have to take their faith outside the church walls and put it into contact with college students. This may happen through service projects, internships, baby-sitting, music, theater, or any number of other projects. Any time college students and mature adults join together there is the potential for a mentoring relationship to develop.

Students seeking a mentoring relationship need to know that a mentor does more than simply pat a person on the back. The mentoring relationship has three basic elements:

> They support, challenge, and provide vision. Through the notion of support, the mentor lets the student know that he or she is understood. Trust must be established; without it the student will not have the courage to move ahead. Challenge creates a gap between the student and the environment. The gap is space for exploration while calling for closure. As the student swings into the abyss of uncertainty, the mentor's vision helps the mentee form his or her own dream. This reflective learning process brings change into consciousness, where it has a chance of remaining a part of the learner. Perhaps it is through this process that students develop a creative spirit, a vision of how the world can be a better place.[3]

Mentoring is not easy. The point is not to make a photocopy of the mentor, but rather to let the student become everything that he or she is destined to be. The mentor helps the mentee develop his or her own goals, establish his or her own direction, and mature into his or her own faith. The formality of the program may come if churches set up a "mentor support group" for people to learn how to be better mentors. But even that can be done informally as mentors meet over lunch or in a Sunday school class.

The mentor relationship is, generally, long term. A student may have a mentor during his or her entire college career. That relationship may very well continue into his or her professional career. This is one of the reasons why there must be mutual benefit. As in any personal relationship, both participants must gain energy from the association.

---

3. R. Lee Evans, "Will Mentoring Undergraduates Inhibit Society Abandonment?" www.auburn.edu/administration/horizon/mentoring.html

To find a person to be a mentor, look for someone you can trust, but someone who is also willing to push you further than you have ever gone. Look for someone who has a mature perspective on life, someone with a mature faith as we defined it in chapter 5. And look for someone who is going somewhere, who has a vision of the future and is moving toward it.

Leadership Development

> When they came, he looked on Eliab and thought, "Surely the Lord's anointed is now before the LORD." But the LORD said to Samuel, "Do not look on his appearance or on the height of his stature, because I have rejected him; for the LORD does not see as mortals see; they look on outward appearance, but the LORD looks on the heart." (1 Sam. 16:6, 7)

The most effective campus ministries are those with strong student leadership. I am convinced that we, as campus ministers, need to let go of our responsibilities as program directors and reclaim our roles as spiritual directors. In a campus ministry with a history of "pastor-as-program-director," that is not an easy transition to make. Each year I have turned over more and more responsibility for this ministry to the students. Each year they have been willing, sometimes even eager, to take that responsibility.

Our leadership structure is fairly simple. We have a student president and chairs of several committees—worship, fellowship, recreation, volunteers, and outreach. We meet as a leadership team each week, alternating between two agendas. One week we look at the specific programs we are doing, the other week we work on developing the team's leadership skills. The president runs the program meeting, I run the leadership training. Both meetings are begun with prayer and Scripture.

Our terms run on a calendar year. We tried going by the school year and decided that we wanted to have experienced leadership over the summer and to begin the fall semester. New leadership team members are selected by the old leadership team. Each committee chair talks with a person whom he or she feels would be interested and would have the time. We really try to listen to God's voice in this process. Sometimes the people we think aren't the best ones for the job end up doing wonderful things.

Our leadership team developed a vision statement and adopted the mission statement from the council (like the board of directors, they oversee the entire ministry). We worked on the vision statement for almost an entire semester:

> Presbyterian Campus Ministry is an innovative community for students to freely explore faith in a welcoming environment. We provide resources and experiences to unleash the leadership potential within each one of us. We provide support and guidance for one another as we identify and carry out our individual ministries. Through our combined ministries we are a diverse community of faith who seek justice, love, kindness, and walk humbly with God.

The vision statement helps us understand where we are going for the long term. It is a statement that will carry us five to ten years down the road, then we will do it all over again. Everything we do is measured by this statement to make sure that it fits in with our overall plan. The mission statement gives us a little more technical detail in saying how we are going to carry out the vision:

> The mission of Presbyterian Campus Ministry is the faith development and nurture of students through programs of Worship, Outreach, Leadership, Fellowship, and Mission so that these students will be a source of strength for the Church and Society.

Both these statements answer the questions of what are we doing and why are we doing it. Clarity of purpose and direction are vital to the life of an organization. The process of developing your own statements is a wonderful experience. It gave us the chance not only to think about where we've been, but to dream about where we are going. It has helped the students take real ownership of this ministry.

Service

> [God] has told you, O mortal, what is good;
>   and what does the LORD require of you
> but to do justice, and to love kindness,
>   and to walk humbly with your God?
>
> —Mic. 6:8

Spring Break Alternatives

It wasn't until my junior year that I really got in touch and it was through the first Spring Break trip that I went on . . . getting in touch with people on campus, a group of friends that were oriented toward social change as some factor in what they wanted to do. Some people who cared. Some people who were aware of what was going on and not just walking with their blinders on. That was a really powerful experience for me. (22-year-old female, senior, uncertain)

■ ■ ■

I began working with spring break alternative trips when I was an adviser for a high school youth group. On one of those trips we were having a discussion about how things were going and what we were learning. A young woman who had been silent for most of the discussion finally spoke up. She said that she had been skeptical about coming on this trip and didn't really see the point. She didn't really care about helping strangers she would never see again. But as this woman began to interact with people she realized how important it was that we do these service projects. She enjoyed getting to know people in a different part of the world and helping with their projects. Her whole life had been changed by this one week-long experience.

We have been sending students on spring break alternative trips every year that I have been at JMU. Every year students return with stories about how their lives have changed. For some the change is subtle. They are a little more aware of the personal aspect of problems they read about in the newspapers. They treat people with a little more respect. For others the change is dramatic. They change their majors. They change their job plans. They change their lifestyle. This is the nature of spring break alternatives.

The design of the trips has changed over the years. We began by sending one group to one location. We sent about fifty students to work in Florida with Habitat for Humanity after Hurricane Andrew ravaged the Homestead area. The next year we sent an even larger group. But the large group was difficult to manage. The students didn't really feel any sense of camaraderie. So the following year we sent small groups to a number of different locations, and that worked much better.

Over the years, we have put an increasing emphasis on student leadership. We now have a training program that meets weekly in October and November. Each group has two or three student leaders who must go through the program to run a trip. They are taught a variety of leadership skills and they are helped with the "nuts and bolts" of the trip, like budget, transportation, meals, and housing.

One of the most important aspects of this program is that Presbyterian Campus Ministry does not run this by itself. We work with Catholic Campus Ministry, the Wesley Foundation, Habitat for Humanity, and JMU's Community Service Learning Center. It is because of this cooperative effort that we are able to attract students who would not go on a "religiously" sponsored trip. What is interesting is the large number of the students who are committed to serving because of their faith, whether that be Christian, Jewish, Muslim, or some other "undefined" belief system.

The other innovation that we have put into the program is the type of work being done. Many folks think of construction when they think of spring break alternatives, but we began two years ago to send students to a variety of other projects. We sent them to work at an AIDS hospice in Miami; an after-school program outside Tallahassee, Florida; a Native American health project in Dulac, Louisiana; an ecology project in the Florida panhandle; a women's shelter in Atlanta; and an inner-city project in Chicago. We also connected a health project with a health sciences class so that students got credit for going on the spring break trip.

Spring break alternatives help students move toward that maturity of faith by giving them confidence in their own beliefs, by helping them gain a respect for others' beliefs, and by helping them see themselves as valuable, contributing members of society. Many of the students still do not want to talk about their faith and how it has been affected by the trip because they do not feel comfortable with the group, so we don't push those conversations. We do try to leave open space so that students who wish to talk about the meanings they are finding can do so.

Fellowship

When I came to JMU, a small Presbyterian Fellowship group met once a week. The campus minister was to do the planning for the group. The students showed up if there wasn't anything else to do. As the semester wore on, the group got smaller and smaller. (This is not unusual for a campus group. Every group at JMU, and probably most other campuses, has the same problem.) I asked the group why they met. They had no idea. They really only met because that is what they had always done.

Groups should have a purpose, even if that purpose is nothing more than to get together and talk about what's happened that week. Without a purpose, people will not make a commitment. With no commitment, no one wants to do any work and the group will finally disappear. It is all right to disband a group. Sometimes it has to be done. I spent several hours every week planning a program. Sometimes people came, sometimes they didn't. I finally got students to take charge of the programs, but still had the same results. It was time to put an end to Wednesday night fellowship.

For one year, we had no fellowship group and that was a huge load off my mind. But I still felt as though we needed something . . . some reason for people to gather and just share life with one another. That is when I had a brainstorm.

LifeSkills Fellowship

People will come to something that fills their needs—perceived or real. Most students know very little about cooking. Most students enjoy a homecooked meal. Put those two needs together and you have LifeSkills Fellowship. I started out teaching the group. I planned a menu, bought the food, and taught the students how to cook it. The group had to be small, only five or six students, because our kitchen was small. I taught them how to cook from scratch—macaroni and cheese, bread, pizza, pancakes, biscuits, turkey, cakes, pies, and cookies. Each semester, the students took a little more responsibility. Last year, they did it all themselves.

LifeSkills has a clearly defined purpose—to teach students how to cook. In that context, they not only learn how to cook, but they develop close friendships while sharing a meal. They share the ups and downs of student life, rejoicing when one gets accepted in a summer job, or mourning when one loses a family member.

Listening Post

So many times we just want someone to listen. We don't need the hassles of an argument or even a debate. We need someone who will help us just get our thoughts out on the table so we can sort through them. I remember a few years ago when I was really struggling with what I should be doing as a campus minister. A minister, a colleague, sat down with me and raked me over the coals for not doing what he thought I should be doing. That was not terribly helpful. It made the confusion worse and made me feel terrible. I really needed someone who would hear me out, help me think through my ideas. Many times in our lives we need a flotation devise. That's what the Listening Post is.

This program, begun in 1979 by Mabel Barth, provides a safe place for students, faculty, and staff just to talk. Barth wanted a place where pain could be acknowledged or high exuberance expressed. She wanted it to be open, easily accessible, without a fee, and with a good listener. This program has quickly spread to colleges and universities all across the United States and around the world. At its most basic, it is a person sitting at a table with a plate of cookies or a bowl of peanuts who will listen to anyone who wants to stop by and talk.

At Elon College in North Carolina, chaplain Richard McBride runs the program using volunteer listeners from a retirement community adjacent to the campus. The Listening Post is open four hours one day each week. Posters are placed around campus to advertise it. The Post is in an easily accessible but somewhat private place in the Campus Center. They do have a logbook to keep track of how many students have stopped by and also to use as a reference in case any follow-up is necessary. With each year, the number of people stopping by has increased.

Not everyone is a good listener right off the bat, so there is a training program for the listeners. The Listening Post manual states, "Probably we have all known individuals who, with or without college experience, somehow make us feel inferior by a showy display of knowledge in an area which we have not had time nor opportunity to explore. Something in their manner makes us feel inept, clod-like. Spontaneity on our part evaporates, and communication dwindles or ceases entirely."[4] The goal of the training is to help people become good listeners—"individuals . . . with whom communication is nearly effortless. When we're with them, it just seems to happen. They can be any adult age: some good listeners are young and zestful; others older and more serious, [all] are equally good communicators. Neither age nor educational experience seems to be the ultimate criterion. It seems to be, instead, a stance toward life."[5]

The manual also includes a basic description of what the Listening Post is and is not.

It is not:

- a traditional counseling center
- a place for "pat" answers
- a place of judgment
- a place with a fee

It is:

- a place for unhurried conversation
- a place to be heard and accepted
- a place to clarify thinking
- a place to consider options
- a place to express human hurt
- a place to be affirmed
- a place to express joy

---

4. From a *Listening Post* information packet.

5. Ibid.

a place to explore ideas
a place to share seemingly impossible dreams
a place of warmth and friendship
a place of gentle challenge toward growth.[6]

The Listening Post is one place where students can try out new ideas to see how they fit. They can wrestle with new dimensions of their life without fear of condemnation. It is a beginning point for some to learn to trust others. It does not have to be religious, though listeners should be prepared to hear about spiritual questions. It may very well be the start of a mentor relationship. At Elon College, a number of students have kept in regular contact with several of the listeners, talking with them "after hours." These listeners provide a sort of island for students, a place to catch their breath before heading back out into the unknown ocean of faith.

For more information about setting up a Listening Post on your campus, contact: The Listening Post, Inc.; 3100 Cherry Creek So. Drive, Suite 1404, Denver, CO 80209-326; phone: (303) 777-7402; e-mail: mbarth@carbon.cudenver.edu.

Coffeehouse

For several years we have run a coffeehouse using a variety of formats and a variety of spaces. We began doing shows—two each during the months of September, October, March, and April—mainly to highlight our singing group, Holy Smoke. Each of the members of Holy Smoke also sang with other folks, so we brought them in as well, creating a show with lots of variety. We also did shows outdoors (that's why only those four months), where we would have lots of students walking by. And we were very successful when the weather allowed. Unfortunately, we were usually only able to do one or two shows each semester. So we looked for a place inside.

We reserved a room in the Student Center twice a month on Friday nights. We asked students, faculty, and staff to perform. The show was free and none of the performers were paid. Some nights we had good audiences, other nights only a handful of folks showed up. But we continued on.

Eventually we moved to a stage built by JMU in the newly constructed wing of the Student Center. There was a sound system, lights, and wonderful coffeeshop-style tables and chairs. Our format

6. Ibid.

became a bit more structured, and, two Fridays a month, we had three acts, each performing for forty-five minutes. The coffeehouse was still free and the performers were not paid.

Last year we decided that the coffeehouse concept was well established in that venue. The university had taken over and was booking student acts almost every night of the week, as well as some paid professional acts. So we agreed to share space with a United Church of Christ congregation in downtown Harrisonburg who also would help us with the coffeehouse. Now we hire both students and nonstudents. We ask for a five-dollar donation at the door and we split that money among the performers. The UCC folks have a sound system and we bring our own lights.

The value of the coffeehouse is that it encourages students to express themselves through music. I am a great believer in the power of music. More than any other art form, music has the ability to reach down into the depths of one's soul and stir things around. Though we do not book specifically "religious" musicians, most of the music performed has a deep spirituality to it.

People need to be responsible for their music. It is too easy to write trash that sells well because it has a popular message about sex, drugs, violence, or alcohol. The message of the music must be a reflection of the life of the musician. It is what gives both the musician and the music integrity. The music and the musicians of the coffeehouse have that integrity. They are life-affirming. They communicate a sense of justice and compassion. They reflect a diversity of styles and cultures.

Here again is an opportunity for faith to grow. Students are challenged with a diversity of ideas and beliefs. The performers can express their own beliefs, which helps them develop an owned faith. They are able to hear the thoughts of older members of the larger community who also perform there.

There are boundaries. We do not invite performers who promote unhealthy lifestyles or attitudes. We do not invite performers who are irresponsible in their actions or their words. This is a place of safety.

There are many ways to provide an open and safe arena for students to explore faith. As I traveled around the country, I found campus ministries and local churches providing a variety of programs and resources that, sometimes without their knowing it, allowed students a time and a place to question their faith and to learn about the faith journeys of others. I would encourage the reader to be creative in developing ideas on the campus and in the congregation that will help students in the shipwreck of faith.

9

Resources

Then the LORD answered me and said:
Write the vision;
    make it plain on tablets,
    so that a runner may read it.
For there is still a vision for the appointed time;
    it speaks of the end, and does not lie.
If it seems to tarry, wait for it;
    it will surely come, it will not delay.

—Hab. 2:2, 3

The gray clouds clutched the mountaintops, blocking the morning sun and leaving a thin film of water on everything. Small patches of fog rolled slowly and silently across the Quad, carrying with it the soft earthy smell of wet leaves and pine needles. The campus was silent this morning. Even the birds must have decided this was a good morning to sleep in.

Todd was standing on the sidewalk waiting to meet Megan so they could go to breakfast together. They were to work on a program for a church youth group about what college life was like. And though the gray mountains in the morning had a beauty all their own, Todd was not noticing it. He wanted to be curled up in his warm, dry bed, his mind journeying through dreamworlds measured not in miles but in heartbeats. He watched as a lone, dark figure approached him.

"Hey, Todd!" spoke a cheery voice from underneath a hooded raincoat. "Isn't it lovely out here?"

"I don't think I can ever get used to these gray fall days," replied Todd with no effort to match Megan's cheerfulness. "You seem in a good mood this morning. What's up with you?"

Megan laughed.

"A very strange chain of events occurred yesterday. I'll tell you about it after we get to the Sandbox."

This, of course, made Todd very curious. He could hardly wait to hear Megan's tale, so he walked quickly down the street, leaving Megan almost running behind him trying to catch up.

When they arrived at the door of the café, Megan was out of breath. Todd held the door so Megan could go in first. The two took off their coats, hung them up on the coatrack, and found a table in the corner.

"So, are you going to tell me what's going on?"

"After we order!"

Todd flung himself back in his seat. Now he was extremely curious. And Megan just kept giving him these strange looks with a knowing smile and an I've-got-a-wonderful-secret sparkle in her eyes.

Arlene came over and set two cups down in front of them. She took their orders, then brought back a pot of coffee and filled their cups. Todd took a sip of the hot coffee, set his cup down, and leaned forward getting closer to Megan.

"OK, tell me what's up."

Megan took her time putting cream and sugar in her cup, stirring it ever so slowly. She knew she was driving Todd crazy. She lifted the cup to her lips and took a several short sips as she watched Todd, relishing his anticipation. Finally she put the cup down.

"Yesterday was almost the end of my time here at Monthaven," she began, watching Todd's eyes open wide in disbelief. "Everything seemed to go wrong all week. I failed two tests, I forgot about a paper that was due. My adviser suggested that I should consider changing my major. Darlene, my roommate, whom I have never gotten along with, was constantly getting on my nerves doing some of the stupidest little things. I just felt as though none of the cogs were meshing. Everything had gotten out of rhythm. I felt like I really didn't belong here. In fact, I felt like I shouldn't even be in college.

"I got so depressed I started thinking about this guy I dated in high school. Our senior year he asked me to marry him. I began to think I should have done that. I should go find him, get married, have some kids. Let my husband take all the responsibility. I'd just stay home."

Todd's mouth had dropped open in total disbelief. He could not believe his ears! But Megan continued.

"The whole thing got worse and worse. The more I thought about it, the more of a nightmare it became. I pictured myself with an apron and bunny rabbit slippers ironing my husband's shirt, a cigarette dangling from my mouth, the TV blaring with *All My Children.* I thought to myself, Maybe that's the best I can do. Maybe that's my life." I got even more depressed. This whole school thing was too much for me. I was too stupid. I could never make the grade. Everything I tried doing was pointless. I felt awful. And all I could do was make myself feel worse."

Megan took a sip from her coffee. She looked out the window at the gray fog drifting lazily down Main Street.

"By Wednesday I had stopped going to classes. I figured there was no point in wasting my time. So I sat around the dorm and watched TV. You know, there are some pretty stupid shows from the sixties and seventies. I mean, *The Courtship of Eddie's Father.* What was that all about? Or *The Partridge Family.* Or how about *My Mother the Car!*

Todd was getting depressed just listening to Megan. He had already lost his appetite. His pancakes sat in front of him getting cold. Arlene wanted to know what was wrong with them.

"Oh, nothing. I've just, uh, you know . . . I've been listening to Megan . . . and uh . . . . "

Arlene took the plate away from him. "I'll put these in the oven for a couple of minutes and warm them up for you. Let me know when you're ready for them."

Arlene knew. She understood about conversations, especially intense ones. She wondered what was going on with Megan, too. She hadn't seen her all week. She was glad she was finally talking to someone.

Todd wanted to hear how things finally got worked out. Megan took another sip of her coffee and leaned forward, her voice almost a whisper.

"Well, I decided to pack things up and leave. Last night, I pulled out my suitcase and started putting clothes in it. I had to get out. I had no idea where I would go. Or where I *could* go. But I knew I couldn't stay. And then Darlene walked in."

Todd liked Darlene. She was always helping him with Habitat projects and she always seemed very enjoyable. He could never understand why she and Megan didn't get along.

"So Darlene sees me packing and she figures I'm going away for the weekend. She sits down and just sort of casually says, 'You know, I really envy you.'

"Well that just about blew me out of the water. She envies me? I had to stop for a minute. I asked her what she meant by that and she said, 'Well, you always seem to be so together. Here you've had this hellacious week, everything going wrong. If it were me, I'd be packing to leave *permanently*. But you, you're just as cool as can be, going to visit friends for the weekend. I don't know how you do it!' I just stared at her. She must have thought I'd lost it."

Todd sat back in his seat shaking his head. He couldn't think of anything to say. All this seemed to have come up out of nowhere. He agreed with Darlene; he always thought Megan was very level-headed, very cool even in the worst crisis. He was hearing about a side of Megan he never imagined was even possible.

Megan pushed her coffee cup to the side and leaned on her elbows.

"I stood there in silence for what seemed like hours. And finally I just lost it and burst into tears. I told Darlene everything that had happened that week and how it made me feel like I was totally worthless. And Darlene was really good. She told me how smart she thought I was and how I could do anything I wanted to. She told me if I ever needed to just dump on somebody, she was there for me. She knew how frustrating school could get, but she really thought I should stick it out. Then she helped me unpack everything. By that time I was so tired I just went to bed.

"Then, this morning, I was just going to blow off this meeting with you. I mean, what was I going to tell a bunch of high school kids about going to college? But for some reason, I couldn't sleep, so I got up. When I looked in the mirror, there was this note. I could barely read it—you know how your eyes don't focus so well first thing in the morning. The note said, 'You can be anybody you want to be. Be the best. Your roommate and your friend, Darlene.' "

■ ■ ■

A little encouragement goes a long way, especially when it comes from an unexpected source. There have been any number of times when I have gotten so frustrated with campus ministry that I felt like just walking away. There have also been any number of times when I have felt like leaving the church and finding another organization that appreciates me. Then I read a book, or have a conversation with someone, or receive a note in the mail that tells me I am doing all right. And that puts me back on my feet and gives me energy to keep on going.

People always want to know what resources are being used in particular ministries. I have been disappointed in how few resources are available specifically for campus ministry. As a result, I have had to adapt some resources from other areas of the church and some from the secular world. Lots of creative ideas are out there. Every time I read something I ask myself, What does this say to campus ministry? The answers have been surprising. So here are some of my favorite resources from which I have gotten both encouragement and vision.

Creativity

A Whack on the Side of the Head, by Roger Von Oech. New York: Warner Books, Inc., 1993. ISBN 0-446-39-158-1.

If you are going to be in the ministry, you have to be creative. It is the only way to survive. I ran across Von Oech's book at a recreation conference in Georgia and found it to be wonderful. He writes with a good sense of humor and a realization that not all of us think we are even slightly creative. This book explores things that can put restraints on our creativity and then makes some suggestions for overcoming those restraints.

General Ministry

Amazing Grace: A Vocabulary of Faith, by Kathleen Norris. New York: Riverhead Books, 1998. ISBN 1-57322-078-7.

Norris grew up in the church, then became disillusioned and left it for a number of years. Sound familiar? She writes about her disillusionment and she writes about what brought her back. She had been troubled by the words of the faith that had no meaning for her. After spending some time in a Benedictine monastery, she began to find those meanings, or perhaps it would be better to say the meanings began finding her. The chapters are, for the most part, short, making this an excellent book for a devotional. Norris uses vivid images to describe her experiences with the words she so eloquently defines.

Net Results, edited by Herb Miller. For subscription information call 1-800-672-1789. Web site address: <www.llano.net/net-results>

This is a monthly magazine focusing on church growth. Every once in a while there is an article specifically about campus ministries, but since I think campus ministries are the cutting edge of the church, almost every article has some application to campus ministries. The magazine follows trends in church attendance, stewardship, worship, and education. Included are quotes from the secular world of business that give insights into how we might also be running our religious organizations and developing ourselves as leaders.

The Seven-Day-a-Week Church, by Lyle E. Schaller. Nashville: Abingdon Press, Nashville, 1992. ISBN 0-687-38144-4.

This is the book that first got me thinking about campus ministry in a different way. We really have to be a seven-day-a-week church on the campus. We have a wide variety of things going on in our ministries and in our buildings (if we have one). This is another one of those books that needs some translating, since it is written for a regular church. For campus ministries that are small and focused on one or two programs, Schaller gives some good information on not just expanding your ministry, but why that might be a good idea. He encourages us to be creative in our approaches to ministry, identifying the needs of the community, not just the needs of the members.

Spiritual Fitness: Everyday Exercises for Body and Soul, by Doris Donnelly. San Francisco: HarperSanFrancisco, 1993. ISBN 0-06-061899-X.

This book is good for campus ministers and ministries. Donnelly helps us see the spirituality in all sorts of common tasks like eating, working, laughing and crying. She encourages us to go to the depths in all of our activities and there we will find connections that will encourage us and support us. This is one of the books I used to help me move away from just "religious" activities to a much broader range of programs in which students are far more interested. Many students, I find, do not have the language to talk about the spirituality of sports, or spending time talking with a friend, but they sense that it is there and they long for affirmation from the church.

Leadership

Developing Dynamic Boards: A Proactive Approach to Building Nonprofit Boards of Directors, by James M. Hardy. Erwin, TN: Essex Press, 1990. ISBN 0-930381-02-5.

If your campus ministry is operating independently from a particular church with a group of people who oversee the budget and the program, then, in all likelihood you are a nonprofit organization. I had never really thought of my council as being a nonprofit board of directors with me as the chief executive officer (CEO), but that is what we are. Hardy explains in easy-to-understand terms the organization of the board, its duties and responsibilities, how to evaluate the work of the board, how to recruit new members, and how to conduct effective meetings. His coverage is thorough and insightful. Most of us have boards who love college students but who don't have much knowledge of how they are to work together. This book will help!

The Fifth Discipline: The Art and Practice of the Learning Organization, by Peter M. Senge. New York: Currency/Doubleday, 1990. ISBN 0-385-26095-4.

I had been really frustrated trying to figure out why students were not getting involved in campus ministry in large numbers. This book helped me see that I needed to look beyond my own organization to begin finding some answers. Senge also helped me understand more about the way organizations should work, in general. We spent a leadership-team session on each discipline and found it most enlightening. This is a long book written for corporate managers, but with a little patience and some translation we have been mining campus-ministry gold for several years.

Joining Together: Group Theory and Group Skills, by David W. Johnson and Frank P. Johnson. Needham Heights, MA: Allyn & Bacon, Inc., 1993. ISBN 0-13-510396-7.

I bought this book when I was attending the Presbyterian School of Christian Education. I was on a tight budget and only bought those books that I thought would be useful after graduation. This book has proven its worth many times over. It is a great resource for understanding small-group dynamics. Since our ministry is based on small groups I refer to it often. Numerous games and exercises are included for helping a small group work together and understand its own dynamics.

Secrets of Motivation: How to Get and Keep Volunteers and Paid Staff, by Sue Vineyard. Downers Grove, IL: Heritage Arts Publishing, 1991. ISBN 0-911029-32-X.

Student leaders are volunteer staff. Sometimes they are paid, but most of the time they are giving their time to the ministry. Their satisfaction needs to be a primary concern of the paid staff and the board of directors. This small book is filled with all sorts of ideas to keep your volunteers coming back without abusing them. It explores why people volunteer and what turns people on and off. It is also good to have your students practice some of these ideas on their committee volunteers!

Sharing the Ministry: A Practical Guide for Transforming Volunteers into Ministers, by Jean Morris Trumbauer. Minneapolis: Augsburg Fortress, 1995. ISBN 0-8066-0280-5

We have just started using this book, but I am already impressed. It is in a loose-leaf notebook and has pages that can be pulled out to photocopy (permission is given for specific pages). Sections include Motivation, Recruiting, Training, and Planning. This is about taking that vision and making it real. Here are the nuts and bolts of making a dream happen.

Transforming Church Boards into Communities of Spiritual Leaders, by Charles M. Olsen. Bethesda, MD: The Alban Institute, Inc., 1995. ISBN 1-56699-148-X.

I felt for a number of years that something was missing from our leadership team meetings, but I couldn't quite put a finger on it. After reading Olsen's book, I discovered that what was missing was spirituality. We get so caught up in taking care of the technical end of the ministry that we forget we have been called by God to be spiritual leaders. Olsen's book offers several ways to put our faith back into our meeting times, making them more worshipful, more meaningful, more fun, and more efficient.

Music

Rise Up Singing: The Group Singing Songbook, edited by Peter Blood and Annie Patterson. Bethlehem, PA: Sing Out Corp., 1988. ISBN 0-9626704-7-2.

This is a wonderful collection of songs new and old. The book is divided into categories like "Creativity," "Friendship," "Hard Times and Blues," and the like. There are over twelve hundred songs in the book ranging from traditional folk to contemporary pop. There is no music notation but guitar chords are included. Also a set of tapes is available so you can hear a verse and a chorus for each song. At the end of each song the name of the singer is listed and the album, tape, or CD on which the song is recorded. A second edition should be out in 1999.

Songs, compiled by Yohann Anderson. San Anselmo, CA: Songs and Creations, Inc., 1992.

I have found this book being used by a lot of youth groups and campus ministries. Most of the songs are religious, though it does have some of the great folk songs like "Blowin' in the Wind," "59th Street Bridge Song," and "Let's Get Together." It also has a lot of hymns. The book is available in several different versions. There is the tune book with melody line and guitar chords. There is the regular songbook (5 1/4" x 8 1/4"), and there is a large print edition. All the editions have guitar chords. Teaching tapes are also available. This book is revised every couple of years with new songs added and some of the old ones taken out. It is a wonderful book!

Recreation

The New Games Book, by the New Games Foundation. New York: Doubleday/Dolphin. ISBN 0-385-12516-X.

If I need a game, this is the first book to which I turn. The New Games folks were some of the first to popularize the "everybody wins" concept. These games can be played hard, but without ever declaring winners and losers. They are fun games, silly games, crazy games. The book divides the games into the numbers needed to play, that is, Games for Two, Games for a Dozen; and then divides each of those sections into Very Active, Active, and Moderate. There is a second book, *More New Games*, that keeps disappearing from my library shelf.

Playfair: Everybody's Guide to Noncompetitive Play, by Matt Weinstein and Joel Goodman. San Luis Obispo, CA: Impact Publications, 1980. ISBN 0-915166-50-X.

This book also has lots of great games in which everybody wins. The thing that makes this book different are the instructions. For folks who are just learning how to lead games (and there is a skill and an art to doing so) this book is immensely helpful. The authors tell you how to introduce the game, then give you instructions about teaching the game. They also have innovative ways for dividing people into groups. Rather than just counting off by twos (ho hum), they might have one group be canoes, one submarines, and another sailboats. Just reading the book gets you excited.

Campus ministers are, in general, a resourceful bunch, so I am sure there are other resources that other ministers would recommend. If you are just trying to get a campus ministry started, first of all, blessings on you! But second, contact other campus ministers around you and ask them what resources they are using.

A wonderful ministry available to us through the hard work of the Rev. Darrell Woomer, the chaplain at Lebanon Valley College, is a campus ministry listserve. You can subscribe to this service by posting a note at majordomo@lvc.edu with the word "subscribe campmin-l" in the body of the note. There is always an interesting discussion going on in this list and loads of resources are shared there.

The journey of faith is one of the most important journeys in our lives, yet it is one that we seem to pay the least attention to. In that first struggle to move from the faith of others to our own "owned" faith we are thrown into the frightening and dangerous chaos of the shipwreck. As terrifying as it may be, it is an adventure that we must take if we want to reach a mature faith. Campus ministries have both the great honor and the great responsibility of preparing and accompanying college students on this most difficult part of their journey. We must recognize and take seriously the need for doubts and questioning. We must provide support for those who are preparing to grow in their faith. This is, after all, what it means to be a child in the family of God.

> God be with you till we meet again;
> When life's perils thick confound you,
> Put His arms unfailing round you:
> God be with you till we meet again.
>
> —Jeremiah E. Rankin,
> "God Be with You Till We Meet Again"

About the Author

Rick Hill has been the Presbyterian campus minister at James Madison University for eight years. Prior to that he did an independent ministry of music and recreation based in Richmond, Virginia. He graduated from Union Theological Seminary in Richmond with an M.Div., and from Presbyterian School of Christian Education with an M.A. in Christian education. His undergraduate degree in speech and theater is from Muskingum College.

Rick has always been an innovator, pushing the boundaries of the church. In his constant desire to make faith real, he brings secular elements into contact with the sacred. He is able to find the holy in the music, art, dance, and recreation of the world, helping people to see that God is active in the common world, alive in the humdrum of daily living. Rick is also a songwriter whose music blurs the lines between Christian and folk.